WhatsApp Marketing

A Step-by-Step Guide for Building a Successful Marketing Strategy to Harness the Power of WhatsApp for Campaigns

Chris Kirton

Table of Contents

Introduction

In today's fast-paced digital world, where instant communication has become the norm, businesses constantly seek innovative ways to connect with their audiences. Among the myriad of social media platforms and communication channels available, WhatsApp stands out as a powerful tool that has revolutionized the way we communicate, both personally and professionally. With over two billion users worldwide, WhatsApp offers a unique opportunity for businesses to engage with customers on a more personal level, building trust, loyalty, and ultimately, driving growth.

"WhatsApp Marketing: A Step-by-Step Guide for Building a Successful Marketing Strategy to Harness the Power of WhatsApp for Campaigns" is designed to equip businesses of all sizes with the knowledge and tools needed to effectively leverage this platform. Whether you're a seasoned marketer looking to diversify your digital strategy or a small business owner aiming to expand your reach, this book will provide you with a comprehensive roadmap to mastering WhatsApp marketing.

Throughout this guide, you will learn how to develop a robust WhatsApp marketing strategy, from setting clear objectives to crafting compelling messages that resonate with your audience. We'll explore the various features of WhatsApp, including broadcast lists, groups, and status updates, and how they can be utilized to create engaging and interactive campaigns. You'll also discover best practices for managing customer relationships, ensuring compliance with privacy regulations, and measuring the success of your efforts.

What sets WhatsApp apart from other marketing channels is its intimate nature—messages are delivered directly to a user's phone, making it a more personal form of communication than traditional social media platforms. This direct access, combined with the platform's high engagement rates, presents an unparalleled opportunity for businesses to connect with their audience in real time.

As you embark on your journey to harness the power of WhatsApp for your marketing campaigns, this book will serve as your trusted companion, providing step-by-step guidance and actionable insights. By the end of this guide, you'll be equipped with the skills and confidence to launch successful WhatsApp campaigns that not only reach your target audience but also foster meaningful connections that drive long-term business success.

Welcome to the world of WhatsApp marketing—where conversations lead to conversions, and relationships are the foundation of growth. Let's get started!

Chapter 1: Introduction to WhatsApp Marketing

The Emergence of WhatsApp as a Marketing Powerhouse

In the dynamic landscape of digital communication, WhatsApp has emerged as a formidable force since its inception in 2009. Initially designed as a straightforward messaging application, it has evolved into a global platform with over two billion active users. This exponential growth underscores WhatsApp's pivotal role in everyday communication, transcending personal interactions to become an essential tool for businesses worldwide. The platform's ubiquity and ease of use make it an attractive channel for marketers aiming to reach a vast and diverse audience. As businesses navigate the complexities of digital marketing, WhatsApp offers a unique blend of accessibility and engagement that is hard to replicate on other platforms.

Advantages of Using WhatsApp for Business

WhatsApp presents several distinct advantages that make it an invaluable asset for marketing strategies. One of its primary benefits is the high engagement rate; messages sent via WhatsApp are typically read within minutes, ensuring that marketing communications reach their audience promptly. This immediacy fosters real-time interactions and quick feedback, allowing businesses to respond swiftly to customer inquiries and market trends. Additionally, WhatsApp's nature enhances the relationship between businesses and customers, promoting trust and loyalty. The platform supports various content types, including text, images, videos, and documents, enabling marketers to create rich and diverse campaigns that cater to different consumer preferences.

Core Features Supporting Marketing Efforts

WhatsApp offers a suite of features specifically designed to support business marketing efforts. The WhatsApp Business app provides tools such as automated greetings, quick replies, and detailed business profiles, which streamline communication and enhance customer experience. Broadcast lists allow businesses to send messages to multiple contacts simultaneously while maintaining a personalized touch, making it easier to disseminate information about promotions, new products, or important updates. Groups can be leveraged to build communities around specific interests or products, facilitating interactive discussions and fostering a sense of belonging among customers. Furthermore, the WhatsApp Business API enables larger enterprises to integrate WhatsApp with their existing CRM systems, automating and scaling their marketing and customer service operations efficiently.

Understanding the WhatsApp User Demographics

A thorough understanding of WhatsApp's user demographics is crucial for crafting effective marketing strategies. The platform boasts a diverse and global user base, encompassing various age groups, genders, and socioeconomic backgrounds. It is particularly popular among younger audiences and in emerging markets where smartphone adoption is rapidly increasing. This demographic diversity allows businesses to target specific segments with tailored messages that resonate with their unique preferences and behaviors. By analyzing user data and engagement patterns, marketers can gain valuable insights into their audience's needs and interests, enabling them to create more relevant and impactful campaigns. Additionally, understanding cultural nuances and regional differences can help in designing localized marketing efforts that better connect with customers on a personal level.

Comparing WhatsApp to Other Marketing Platforms

When compared to other digital marketing channels, WhatsApp offers unique strengths that set it apart. Unlike social media platforms where content visibility is often governed by algorithms, WhatsApp ensures direct delivery of messages to users' devices, guaranteeing higher visibility and engagement. The platform's end-to-end encryption provides a secure environment for communication, enhancing customer trust and confidence in sharing personal information. Moreover, WhatsApp's real-time messaging capabilities allow for immediate interactions, making it an ideal platform for time-sensitive promotions, customer support, and instant feedback. These attributes make WhatsApp a more personal and effective channel for building meaningful relationships with customers compared to traditional email marketing or broader social media advertising.

The Evolution of WhatsApp Business Tools

WhatsApp has continually evolved to better serve the needs of businesses, introducing advanced tools and features that enhance marketing and customer engagement. The WhatsApp Business API, for example, allows larger enterprises to automate and manage their communications at scale, integrating seamlessly with existing business systems and workflows. Newer features such as interactive buttons, rich media messages, and chatbots enable businesses to create more engaging and efficient customer interactions. Additionally, WhatsApp is expanding its e-commerce capabilities, allowing businesses to showcase products and facilitate transactions directly within the app. These ongoing developments demonstrate WhatsApp's commitment to supporting businesses in their marketing endeavors, ensuring that the platform remains a cutting-edge tool in the digital marketing arsenal.

WhatsApp Marketing represents a significant advancement in the way businesses connect with their audiences. Its extensive reach, high engagement rates, and versatile features provide a powerful platform for creating personalized and effective marketing campaigns. By understanding the unique advantages of WhatsApp, leveraging its core features, and tailoring strategies to fit the diverse user demographics, businesses can harness the full potential of this communication giant. As digital marketing continues to evolve, WhatsApp stands out as a key channel for building deeper connections, fostering customer loyalty, and driving sustainable business growth. This chapter has laid the foundation for exploring the strategic implementation of WhatsApp in marketing campaigns, setting the stage for the detailed guidance that follows in the subsequent chapters.

1.1 Understanding the Role of WhatsApp in Modern Marketing

The Shift from Traditional to Digital Marketing

The evolution from traditional marketing methods to digital channels has reshaped how businesses communicate with consumers. Traditional marketing, characterized by print ads, television commercials, and direct mail, relied heavily on broad messaging aimed at a wide audience. While effective in its time, these methods often lacked the immediacy and personalization that modern consumers now expect. The rise of the internet and mobile technology has led to a significant shift towards digital marketing, where platforms like social media, email, and messaging apps have become the primary channels for engaging with customers. Among these digital tools, WhatsApp has emerged as a critical player, offering a unique blend of personal communication and mass outreach that bridges the gap between traditional and digital marketing approaches.

WhatsApp's Global Reach and Penetration

WhatsApp's widespread adoption across the globe makes it a vital platform for businesses looking to expand their reach. With over two billion users in more than 180 countries, WhatsApp offers unparalleled access to a diverse and extensive audience. Its penetration is particularly strong in emerging markets, where the app has become a staple of daily communication. This global reach allows businesses to target both local and international markets with relative ease, enabling them to tailor their marketing efforts to specific regions or demographics. The platform's popularity across different age groups and socioeconomic backgrounds further enhances its value as a marketing tool, providing opportunities to engage with a broad spectrum of potential customers.

The Role of Instant Messaging in Consumer Behavior

The advent of instant messaging has profoundly influenced consumer behavior, with WhatsApp playing a central role in this transformation. Instant messaging has become the preferred mode of communication for many consumers, offering convenience, speed, and a sense of immediacy that other forms of communication often lack. This shift in behavior has significant implications for businesses, as consumers now expect real-time interactions with brands. WhatsApp, with its instant messaging capabilities, allows businesses to meet these expectations by providing immediate responses to customer inquiries, facilitating quick transactions, and delivering timely updates. This immediacy not only enhances customer satisfaction but also fosters a stronger connection between the brand and the consumer.

WhatsApp as a Tool for Personalized Marketing

Personalization has become a cornerstone of effective marketing in the digital age, and WhatsApp excels in facilitating personalized communication. Unlike other marketing channels that often rely on one-size-fits-all messages, WhatsApp allows businesses to tailor their communications to individual customers. By leveraging WhatsApp's direct messaging features, businesses can send personalized offers, recommendations, and updates that resonate with the specific needs and preferences of each customer. This level of personalization helps to build stronger relationships, as customers feel valued and understood by the brand. Moreover, the ability to engage in two-way conversations on WhatsApp enables businesses to gather valuable insights into customer behavior and preferences, further enhancing the personalization of their marketing efforts.

Enhancing Customer Engagement and Retention

One of WhatsApp's most significant contributions to modern marketing is its ability to enhance customer engagement and retention. The platform's interactive nature encourages active participation from customers, whether through direct conversations, group discussions, or engagement with multimedia content. This interactive environment fosters a sense of community and loyalty among customers, making them more likely to engage with the brand over the long term. Additionally, WhatsApp's features, such as broadcast lists and status updates, provide businesses with multiple touchpoints to maintain regular communication with their audience. By consistently delivering relevant and valuable content, businesses can keep their brand top of mind, ultimately leading to higher customer retention rates.

Integrating WhatsApp with Broader Marketing Strategies

While WhatsApp is a powerful marketing tool in its own right, its true potential is unlocked when integrated with broader marketing strategies. Businesses can use WhatsApp to complement their efforts on other digital channels, such as social media, email marketing, and websites. For example, WhatsApp can be used to drive traffic to a company's website, provide instant customer support for social media campaigns, or send personalized follow-ups to email marketing subscribers. By integrating WhatsApp into a cohesive marketing strategy, businesses can create a seamless and unified customer experience across multiple touchpoints. This integration not only amplifies the effectiveness of individual marketing efforts but also helps to build a more comprehensive and connected brand presence.

Understanding the role of WhatsApp in modern marketing is essential for businesses aiming to thrive in today's digital landscape. The platform's global reach, ability to facilitate instant and personalized communication, and capacity to enhance customer engagement make it an invaluable asset for any marketing strategy. As businesses continue to navigate the complexities of digital marketing, WhatsApp offers a unique opportunity to connect with customers in meaningful and impactful ways. By embracing WhatsApp as a central component of their marketing efforts, businesses can leverage its strengths to drive growth, foster loyalty, and create lasting relationships with their audience.

1.2 Why WhatsApp? Advantages Over Other Platforms

Unmatched Global Reach and User Engagement

One of the most compelling reasons to choose WhatsApp over other platforms is its unparalleled global reach. With over two billion active users worldwide, WhatsApp has established itself as a dominant force in the realm of instant messaging. Unlike other platforms that may have strong user bases in specific regions or demographics, WhatsApp's penetration is truly global, making it an ideal tool for businesses looking to connect with a diverse and expansive audience. This widespread adoption translates into high user engagement, with most messages read and responded to within minutes. This level of engagement is critical for marketers who need to ensure that their messages are not only delivered but also promptly acted upon.

Direct and Personal Communication Channel

WhatsApp offers a level of directness and personalization that is difficult to achieve on other platforms. Unlike social media channels, where content is often filtered through algorithms and may or may not reach the intended audience, WhatsApp delivers messages directly to users' devices. This direct communication channel allows businesses to engage with customers on a more personal level, fostering a sense of intimacy and trust. The ability to send personalized messages tailored to individual customer preferences further enhances this connection. Whether it's sending a special offer, providing customer support, or simply staying in touch, WhatsApp enables businesses to create meaningful interactions that can lead to stronger customer relationships and higher loyalty.

High Message Open and Response Rates

One of the key advantages of WhatsApp over other marketing platforms is its exceptionally high message open and response rates. Studies have shown that WhatsApp messages have an open rate of around 98%, far surpassing the open rates of email marketing, which typically hovers between 20% and 30%. This high open rate means that businesses can be confident that their messages are being seen by their audience. Moreover, the response rate on WhatsApp is also significantly higher than on other platforms, with users more likely to engage in conversations and provide immediate feedback. This responsiveness is particularly valuable for businesses that need to communicate time-sensitive information or require quick customer interactions.

Secure and Encrypted Communication

In an era where data privacy is of paramount concern, WhatsApp stands out for its commitment to security. The platform offers end-to-end encryption for all messages, ensuring that only the sender and recipient can read the contents. This level of security is a major advantage for businesses, particularly those dealing with sensitive information or in industries where privacy is crucial, such as finance or healthcare. Encrypted communication not only protects customer data but also enhances trust between the business and its customers. Unlike some other platforms where security breaches and data leaks are common, WhatsApp's robust encryption provides peace of mind for both businesses and their clients.

Cost-Effective Marketing Solution

WhatsApp is a highly cost-effective solution for businesses, particularly when compared to traditional advertising channels or other digital platforms. The app itself is free to use, and businesses can communicate with customers at no additional cost, aside from the internet data required. This affordability makes WhatsApp an attractive option for small businesses or startups with limited marketing budgets. Additionally, the high engagement rates on WhatsApp mean that businesses can achieve a greater return on investment (ROI) compared to other platforms where paid advertising is often necessary to reach a significant audience. By leveraging WhatsApp's features effectively, businesses can conduct marketing campaigns, provide customer service, and even close sales without incurring substantial costs.

Versatile Media Sharing Capabilities

WhatsApp's versatility in media sharing is another key advantage over other platforms. Businesses can send a variety of media types, including text messages, images, videos, voice notes, documents, and even location data. This multimedia capability allows for creative and dynamic marketing campaigns that can capture the attention of users in different ways. For example, a business might use video messages to showcase new products, send images of promotional flyers, or share PDFs of product catalogs. The ability to convey information through multiple formats enhances the overall communication experience and helps businesses to better engage with their audience. Additionally, WhatsApp's support for rich media makes it easier to create compelling content that resonates with users.

Integration with Business Systems and Automation

WhatsApp's ability to integrate with existing business systems and support automation is a significant advantage for larger enterprises. Through the WhatsApp Business API, companies can connect the platform with their customer relationship management (CRM) systems, enabling seamless communication and data management. This integration allows businesses to automate various aspects of their customer interactions, such as sending out automated responses, managing customer inquiries, and even processing orders. The API also supports chatbots, which can handle routine customer service tasks, freeing up human resources for more complex interactions. This level of integration and automation not only improves efficiency but also enhances the overall customer experience by providing timely and relevant responses.

WhatsApp's unique combination of global reach, direct communication, high engagement rates, security, cost-effectiveness, versatile media capabilities, and integration with business systems makes it a superior choice for modern marketing strategies. While other platforms offer valuable tools, WhatsApp's advantages in these key areas set it apart as a powerful and versatile marketing channel. For businesses looking to build strong, personalized connections with their customers and drive impactful marketing campaigns, WhatsApp offers a platform that is not only effective but also aligned with the needs and expectations of today's digital-savvy consumers.

1.3 Key Statistics and Trends in WhatsApp Marketing

Global User Base and Market Penetration

WhatsApp has solidified its position as the world's leading messaging platform, boasting over two billion active users as of 2024. This extensive user base spans more than 180 countries, making WhatsApp one of the most universally adopted communication tools globally. Notably, the platform's market penetration is particularly strong in regions such as India, Brazil, and parts of Europe, where it has become the primary mode of communication. In India alone, WhatsApp has over 500 million users, making it the most popular app in the country. This widespread adoption is a significant advantage for businesses aiming to reach a global audience, providing them with direct access to a massive and engaged user base.

Engagement Rates and User Behavior

WhatsApp's engagement rates are among the highest in the digital communication landscape, with messages on the platform achieving an average open rate of 98%. This is significantly higher than the open rates seen on other channels, such as email, where the average is around 20%. Additionally, the response rate on WhatsApp is impressive, with users often replying to messages within minutes. This immediacy is driven by the platform's role as a primary communication tool, where users check their messages multiple times throughout the day. Businesses leveraging WhatsApp for marketing can therefore expect quick and direct engagement with their audience, a crucial factor for time-sensitive campaigns and customer service interactions.

WhatsApp Business App Usage

Since its launch in 2018, the WhatsApp Business app has seen rapid adoption among small and medium-sized enterprises (SMEs). As of 2024, over 200 million businesses worldwide are actively using the app to communicate with their customers. The WhatsApp Business app offers a range of features tailored to business needs, such as automated greetings, quick replies, and detailed analytics. These tools help businesses manage customer interactions efficiently while providing valuable insights into customer behavior and preferences. The high adoption rate of the WhatsApp Business app highlights its effectiveness as a marketing tool, particularly for SMEs looking to build personal connections with their customers without the need for significant investment in complex customer relationship management (CRM) systems.

Growth of WhatsApp Business API Adoption

The WhatsApp Business API, designed for larger enterprises, has also seen substantial growth. As companies recognize the value of integrating WhatsApp into their broader customer engagement strategies, the adoption of the API has surged. The API allows businesses to automate and scale their communications, making it possible to handle high volumes of customer interactions seamlessly. This is particularly valuable for businesses in industries such as e-commerce, where real-time communication can significantly impact customer satisfaction and sales conversions. The growing adoption of the WhatsApp Business API is a clear indicator of the platform's importance in the enterprise sector, enabling businesses to deliver personalized, timely, and efficient customer service at scale.

Impact on Customer Satisfaction and Loyalty

Statistics indicate that businesses using WhatsApp as part of their customer service strategy report higher levels of customer satisfaction and loyalty. According to a study by Facebook, 67% of users say they would prefer to communicate with businesses via messaging rather than phone or email. WhatsApp's ease of use and the immediacy of responses contribute to a more satisfying customer experience, leading to increased customer retention rates. Furthermore, businesses that engage with their customers on WhatsApp are seen as more accessible and responsive, traits that are highly valued in today's competitive marketplace. This positive impact on customer satisfaction underscores the importance of WhatsApp as a tool for building long-term customer relationships.

Emerging Trends in WhatsApp Marketing

Several emerging trends are shaping the future of WhatsApp marketing. One notable trend is the increasing use of multimedia content in marketing campaigns. With WhatsApp supporting various media formats such as videos, images, and voice messages, businesses are leveraging these features to create more engaging and interactive campaigns. Another trend is the rise of conversational commerce, where businesses use WhatsApp to facilitate transactions and provide personalized shopping experiences directly within the app. Additionally, the integration of artificial intelligence (AI) and chatbots is becoming more prevalent, allowing businesses to offer 24/7 customer support and automate routine interactions. These trends reflect the evolving nature of WhatsApp marketing, as businesses seek to maximize the platform's potential in innovative ways.

Regional Trends and Cultural Preferences

Understanding regional trends and cultural preferences is crucial for businesses using WhatsApp for marketing. In regions like Latin America and Southeast Asia, where WhatsApp is deeply ingrained in daily communication, businesses are increasingly using the platform for community-building and localized marketing efforts. For instance, in Brazil, WhatsApp has become a primary tool for small businesses to reach local customers, with many businesses relying on the app to manage orders and customer inquiries. Cultural preferences also play a significant role in shaping how businesses use WhatsApp. In some regions, users prefer more visual content, while in others, text-based communication is more effective. Tailoring marketing strategies to align with these regional trends and cultural nuances can significantly enhance the effectiveness of WhatsApp marketing campaigns.

The key statistics and trends in WhatsApp marketing underscore the platform's powerful role in modern business communication. With its vast global reach, high engagement rates, and growing adoption among businesses, WhatsApp has become an indispensable tool for marketers. The emerging trends in multimedia content, conversational commerce, and AI-driven interactions highlight the platform's dynamic nature and its innovation potential. By understanding these statistics and trends, businesses can better leverage WhatsApp to create effective marketing strategies that resonate with their audience, drive customer satisfaction, and foster long-term loyalty. As WhatsApp continues to evolve, it is poised to remain at the forefront of digital marketing, offering businesses new and exciting opportunities to connect with their customers.

Chapter 2: Setting Up WhatsApp for Business

Choosing the Right WhatsApp Solution

The first step in setting up WhatsApp for your business is choosing the right solution that aligns with your operational needs. WhatsApp offers two primary solutions for businesses: the WhatsApp Business app and the WhatsApp Business API. The WhatsApp Business app is designed for small and medium-sized enterprises (SMEs) and provides essential features such as business profiles, automated replies, and message statistics. It is user-friendly and suitable for businesses that do not require advanced integrations or high-volume messaging capabilities.

In contrast, the WhatsApp Business API is geared towards larger enterprises or businesses with higher messaging volumes. It offers advanced features such as integration with customer relationship management (CRM) systems, automation through chatbots, and the ability to manage multiple user accounts from a centralized platform. Choosing between the WhatsApp Business app and the WhatsApp Business API depends on factors such as the size of your business, your messaging needs, and your technical resources.

Creating and Configuring Your WhatsApp Business Account

Once you have selected the appropriate WhatsApp solution, the next step is to create and configure your WhatsApp Business account. For the WhatsApp Business app, download the application from your device's app store and follow the setup instructions. You will need to register your business phone number, which will be used for all communications through the app. It's essential to use a phone number that is dedicated to your business to ensure seamless communication and maintain professionalism.

After registering your phone number, complete your business profile by providing essential information such as your business name, description, address, and website. You can also add a business profile picture that represents your brand, such as your logo. Configuring your business profile effectively is crucial for establishing credibility and ensuring that customers have all the necessary information to connect with you.

For businesses opting for the WhatsApp Business API, the setup process involves additional steps. You will need to apply for API access through the WhatsApp Business API provider or directly through WhatsApp. This process may involve verification of your business and phone number, as well as integration with your existing systems. Once approved, you will configure your API settings, including your messaging templates, automated responses, and CRM integrations.

Setting Up Automated Messaging Features

Automated messaging features are a key component of the WhatsApp Business app and API, enhancing your ability to manage customer interactions efficiently. For the WhatsApp Business app, you can set up automated greetings, quick replies, and away messages. Automated greetings can be sent to new customers or when they first message your business, providing a warm welcome and basic information about your services. Quick replies allow you to create pre-defined responses for frequently asked questions, saving time and ensuring consistency in your communications.

Away messages are useful for informing customers when you are not available, such as outside of business hours or during holidays. These messages can be customized to provide alternative contact methods or inform customers when they can expect a response. By utilizing these automated messaging features, you can improve response times and maintain a high level of customer service even when you are not actively available.

For businesses using the WhatsApp Business API, automation capabilities extend further. You can set up complex workflows and integrate chatbots to handle routine customer interactions, process orders, and provide support. Automated messaging templates can be created for various scenarios, such as order confirmations, appointment reminders, and promotional offers. These templates must be approved by WhatsApp to ensure they meet the platform's guidelines and maintain a high standard of customer experience.

Integrating WhatsApp with Your Business Systems

Integrating WhatsApp with your existing business systems can significantly enhance your operational efficiency and customer experience. For the WhatsApp Business app, integration options are relatively limited, but you can use third-party tools to connect with your customer support and marketing platforms. These integrations can help synchronize customer data and streamline communication processes.

For larger businesses using the WhatsApp Business API, integration with CRM systems and other business tools is a core feature. By connecting WhatsApp with your CRM, you can manage customer interactions, track conversations, and access valuable data insights from a centralized dashboard. Integration with e-commerce platforms allows you to facilitate transactions and provide real-time order updates directly through WhatsApp. Additionally, connecting with marketing automation tools enables you to run targeted campaigns and measure their effectiveness. These integrations help create a seamless customer experience and ensure that all aspects of your business communication are synchronized.

Managing Contacts and Communication Preferences

Effectively managing contacts and communication preferences is essential for maintaining organized and personalized interactions with your customers. In the WhatsApp Business app, you can categorize your contacts into different groups based on their engagement or interests. This categorization helps you tailor your messages and manage communication more efficiently.

Additionally, you can set communication preferences for each contact or group, specifying how and when you want to interact with them. For example, you can choose to send promotional messages to specific groups while reserving direct customer support for individual contacts. Managing these preferences ensures that your communications are relevant and well-targeted, enhancing customer satisfaction.

For businesses using the WhatsApp Business API, managing contacts and communication preferences involves more advanced features. You can segment your audience based on various criteria and automate personalized messaging campaigns. CRM integration allows you to maintain detailed profiles for each customer, track their interactions, and tailor your communication based on their preferences and behavior.

Monitoring and Analyzing Performance

Monitoring and analyzing the performance of your WhatsApp communications is crucial for optimizing your marketing strategy and improving customer interactions. The WhatsApp Business app provides basic analytics features, including metrics on message delivery, read rates, and response times. These insights help you gauge the effectiveness of your messaging and identify areas for improvement.

For businesses using the WhatsApp Business API, performance monitoring is more comprehensive. You can access detailed analytics on message performance, customer engagement, and campaign effectiveness. Integration with analytics platforms allows you to track key performance indicators (KPIs) and generate reports to evaluate the success of your WhatsApp marketing efforts. By analyzing these metrics, you can make data-driven decisions, refine your strategies, and enhance overall customer experience.

Setting up WhatsApp for business involves several key steps, including choosing the right solution, configuring your account, and utilizing automated messaging features. Whether you use the WhatsApp Business app or the WhatsApp Business API, integrating WhatsApp with your business systems and managing communication preferences effectively are essential for maximizing the platform's potential. Monitoring and analyzing performance metrics further allows you to optimize your strategies and ensure that your WhatsApp communications are delivering value to your customers. By following these guidelines, you can establish a robust WhatsApp presence that enhances customer engagement and drives business growth.

2.1 Choosing the Right WhatsApp Platform: Business App vs. API

WhatsApp Business App: Ideal for Small to Medium-Sized Enterprises

The WhatsApp Business app is designed specifically for small to medium-sized enterprises (SMEs) that need a straightforward, cost-effective solution for managing customer communications. It provides a range of features tailored to help businesses engage with their customers effectively while keeping overhead costs low.

Key Features:

- **Business Profile**: Create a detailed business profile with essential information such as your business name, description, address, and website. This profile helps customers find and learn more about your business.
- **Automated Messages**: Set up automated greetings, away messages, and quick replies. These features help streamline communication, respond to common queries quickly, and ensure customers are informed about your availability.
- **Labels**: Organize your contacts with labels to categorize them based on interactions or characteristics, such as "New Leads" or "VIP Customers." This helps manage communication more effectively and tailor your messages.
- **Message Statistics**: Access basic analytics, including message delivery, read rates, and response times. These insights help you understand how your messages are performing and identify areas for improvement.

Pros:

- **Cost-Effective**: The WhatsApp Business app is free to use, making it an attractive option for businesses with limited budgets.

- **Ease of Use**: It is user-friendly and does not require advanced technical knowledge to set up or manage.
- **Quick Setup**: Businesses can get started quickly by simply downloading the app and registering a business phone number.

Cons:

- **Limited Scalability**: The app is best suited for businesses with moderate messaging needs. It may not be adequate for companies with high messaging volumes or complex communication requirements.
- **Basic Integration**: Integration with other business systems and CRM platforms is limited, which might restrict the app's functionality for some businesses.

WhatsApp Business API: Designed for Larger Enterprises

The WhatsApp Business API is tailored for larger enterprises or businesses with significant communication needs. It offers advanced features and greater flexibility, making it suitable for high-volume messaging and integration with existing business systems.

Key Features:

- **Advanced Integration**: Integrate with CRM systems, e-commerce platforms, and other business tools. This allows for seamless data synchronization, enhanced customer management, and streamlined operations.

- **Automation and Chatbots**: Utilize chatbots and automated workflows to handle routine customer interactions, process orders, and provide real-time support. This can significantly reduce manual effort and improve efficiency.
- **Customizable Messaging**: Create and use message templates for various scenarios, such as order confirmations or appointment reminders. These templates must be pre-approved by WhatsApp, ensuring compliance with their guidelines.
- **Multiple User Accounts**: Manage multiple users and departments from a centralized platform, making it easier to coordinate communication across your organization.

Pros:

- **Scalability**: The API supports high messaging volumes and complex communication needs, making it ideal for large enterprises.
- **Enhanced Functionality**: Advanced features and integrations provide a comprehensive solution for managing customer interactions and data.
- **Custom Solutions**: Tailor your communication strategy with greater flexibility, including custom integrations and automated processes.

Cons:

- **Cost**: The WhatsApp Business API often involves additional costs, including setup fees from API providers. This may be a consideration for businesses with smaller budgets.
- **Complex Setup**: Implementing and managing the API requires technical expertise and may involve a longer setup process compared to the WhatsApp Business app.
- **Approval Process**: Message templates and certain features require approval from WhatsApp, which can introduce delays and additional compliance requirements.

Making the Right Choice for Your Business

Choosing between the WhatsApp Business app and the WhatsApp Business API depends on several factors, including the size of your business, your messaging volume, and your technical capabilities.

- **For Small to Medium-Sized Businesses**: The WhatsApp Business app is a practical solution if you are looking for a cost-effective way to manage customer interactions without needing complex integrations or handling high messaging volumes. It offers essential features to help you engage with your customers efficiently and is easy to set up and use.
- **For Large Enterprises**: The WhatsApp Business API is more suitable if you require advanced functionality, high scalability, and seamless integration with other business systems. It supports extensive automation, customizable messaging, and high-volume interactions, making it ideal for larger organizations with more complex communication needs.

Consider your specific business requirements and resources when making your decision. Both platforms offer valuable tools for enhancing customer communication, but selecting the right one ensures that you can effectively meet your business goals and provide a positive customer experience.

2.2 Creating a Professional Business Profile

Importance of a Professional Business Profile

A well-crafted business profile on WhatsApp is crucial for establishing credibility and making a strong first impression with your customers. It serves as the face of your business on the platform, providing essential information and setting the tone for interactions. A professional profile not only helps in building trust but also ensures that customers can easily find and contact your business.

Steps to Create a Professional Business Profile

1. Register a Dedicated Business Phone Number

Start by registering a phone number that is exclusively used for your business. This number should be different from your phone number to maintain professionalism and ensure that all business communications are kept separate from personal interactions. Choose a number that is easy for customers to remember and is consistent with your existing contact details, such as your website or business cards.

2. Choose a Business Name

Select a clear and recognizable business name for your WhatsApp profile. This name should reflect your brand identity and be easily identifiable by your customers. Avoid using abbreviations or complex names that may confuse customers. Consistency is key, so use the same business name across all your communication channels to build brand recognition.

3. Write a Compelling Business Description

Craft a concise and informative business description that highlights what your business does and what makes it unique. Your description should be engaging and convey the value you offer to your customers. Include relevant keywords that potential customers might use when searching for services or products you provide. Keep the description brief but informative, focusing on your core services or products.

4. Add Business Details

Provide essential business details such as your physical address, website URL, and business hours. Including your address helps customers find your location, while the website URL allows them to access more information about your business. Clearly state your business hours so customers know when they can expect to reach you. If you operate in multiple locations or have different departments, consider including this information to help customers connect with the right part of your business.

5. Select an Appropriate Profile Picture

Choose a profile picture that represents your brand professionally. This could be your business logo, a high-quality image of your storefront, or another visual element that reflects your business identity. Ensure the image is clear and easily recognizable, even when displayed at a smaller size on mobile devices. A professional profile picture helps build trust and makes your profile more visually appealing.

6. Set Up Business Categories

WhatsApp allows you to select business categories that best describe your business. Choose categories that accurately reflect the nature of your business and the services or products you offer. This categorization helps potential customers understand what your business is about and improves the chances of being found by users searching for related services.

7. Enable and Customize Automated Messages

Leverage automated messaging features to enhance your business profile. Set up automated greetings to welcome new customers and provide a brief introduction to your business. Configure away messages to inform customers when you are not available, and set up quick replies for frequently asked questions. These automated messages ensure timely communication and improve customer experience by providing immediate responses.

8. Maintain Consistency and Update Regularly

Regularly review and update your business profile to ensure that all information remains accurate and current. If there are changes to your business hours, address, or services, make sure to update your profile accordingly. Consistency in your profile information across all platforms helps maintain a professional image and ensures that customers receive reliable and up-to-date information.

Best Practices for a Professional Business Profile

- **Keep It Professional**: Ensure that all elements of your business profile, including the name, description, and profile picture, reflect a professional image.
- **Be Clear and Concise**: Straightforwardly provide essential information. Avoid jargon or overly complex language that may confuse customers.
- **Engage with Customers**: Use your profile to create a welcoming and engaging presence. Encourage customers to reach out with inquiries and respond promptly to their messages.
- **Monitor and Improve**: Regularly review your profile's performance and gather feedback from customers. Use this information to make improvements and enhance your profile's effectiveness.

Creating a professional business profile on WhatsApp is a foundational step in establishing a strong presence on the platform. By carefully selecting your business name, writing a compelling description, and providing essential details, you create a profile that enhances credibility and fosters trust with your customers. Utilizing automated messaging features and maintaining consistency ensures that your profile remains effective and up-to-date. A well-crafted business profile not only helps in attracting and engaging customers but also sets the stage for successful interactions and business growth.

2.3 Building Your Contact List: Best Practices

The Importance of a Targeted Contact List

In WhatsApp marketing, the quality of your contact list is far more important than its size. A well-curated, targeted contact list allows you to engage with potential and existing customers who are genuinely interested in your products or services. This results in higher engagement rates, more effective campaigns, and ultimately, better business outcomes. Building a contact list strategically ensures that your communications are relevant and welcomed, reducing the risk of being marked as spam or facing compliance issues.

Obtaining Consent and Compliance with Regulations

Before you start adding contacts to your list, it's crucial to obtain explicit consent from individuals. WhatsApp marketing is permission-based, meaning that people must opt-in to receive messages from your business. This consent can be obtained through various channels such as your website, social media, or during in-person interactions. Make sure to clearly explain what kind of messages they will receive, such as promotions, updates, or customer support communications.

Compliance with regulations like the General Data Protection Regulation (GDPR) in Europe or the CAN-SPAM Act in the United States is essential. These laws require businesses to respect users' privacy and provide them with control over their data. Always offer an easy way for contacts to opt out of your messages if they choose to, and ensure that you are transparent about how their data will be used.

Leveraging Existing Customer Data

Your existing customer database is a valuable resource for building your WhatsApp contact list. If you have already obtained consent from customers to communicate with them via messaging platforms, you can invite them to join your WhatsApp contact list. This can be done through an email campaign, a prompt on your website, or through in-store signage. Encourage customers to add your business number to their contacts and opt-in for updates or exclusive offers via WhatsApp.

When integrating existing customer data, it's important to segment your list based on customer behavior, preferences, and purchase history. This segmentation allows you to tailor your messages to different groups, ensuring that your communications are relevant and personalized. For example, you might have separate lists for new customers, repeat buyers, and those who haven't engaged with your business in a while.

Using Opt-In Forms on Digital Platforms

Opt-in forms are an effective way to grow your WhatsApp contact list online. These forms can be placed on various digital platforms, such as your website, blog, or landing pages. To encourage sign-ups, offer an incentive, such as a discount code, free content, or exclusive access to promotions. The opt-in form should be simple, with clear instructions on how customers can sign up and what they can expect from your WhatsApp communications.

Ensure that your opt-in forms are mobile-friendly, as many users will be accessing them from their smartphones. You can also include a checkbox allowing users to agree to receive messages via WhatsApp, ensuring that you obtain explicit consent. Integrate these forms with your customer relationship management (CRM) system to automate the process of adding new contacts to your list and sending them a welcome message on WhatsApp.

Promoting Your WhatsApp Channel on Social Media

Social media platforms like Facebook, Instagram, and Twitter are powerful tools for promoting your WhatsApp channel and growing your contact list. You can share your WhatsApp business number or a direct link to your WhatsApp chat on your social media profiles, encouraging followers to connect with you on WhatsApp. Running targeted ads or campaigns that highlight the benefits of joining your WhatsApp list, such as receiving exclusive offers or early access to new products, can also be effective.

Utilize WhatsApp's click-to-chat feature, which allows users to start a conversation with your business by simply clicking a link or button on your social media pages. This feature removes the friction of having to manually save your number, making it easier for users to connect with you. Incorporating a call-to-action in your social media posts, such as "Chat with us on WhatsApp" or "Get updates directly on WhatsApp," can drive more sign-ups.

Encouraging Sign-Ups through Offline Channels

While digital methods are essential, don't overlook the power of offline channels to grow your WhatsApp contact list. If you have a physical store, restaurant, or service location, you can encourage customers to join your WhatsApp list at the point of sale. Displaying your WhatsApp number on receipts, in-store signage, or business cards invites customers to connect with you after their visit. Offering a small incentive, such as a discount on their next purchase for joining your WhatsApp list, can be a great motivator.

During events, trade shows, or workshops, you can also promote your WhatsApp channel by including your business number on promotional materials or having a sign-up booth where attendees can opt-in. If you collect business cards or contact details at these events, be sure to follow up with an invitation to join your WhatsApp list, always emphasizing the value they'll receive by staying connected.

Maintaining and Cleaning Your Contact List

Building a contact list is not a one-time task; it requires ongoing maintenance to keep it effective. Regularly review your contact list to ensure that it remains up-to-date and relevant. Remove inactive contacts who haven't engaged with your messages for an extended period, as they may no longer be interested in your offerings. This process, known as list cleaning, helps improve your engagement rates and ensures that your messages are reaching a receptive audience.

Additionally, monitor the performance of your WhatsApp campaigns and use analytics to understand which segments of your contact list are most responsive. This data can guide your efforts in refining your list and focusing on the most valuable contacts. By keeping your list well-maintained and relevant, you'll enhance the effectiveness of your WhatsApp marketing strategy and maximize the return on your efforts.

Building a high-quality contact list is a critical component of successful WhatsApp marketing. By obtaining explicit consent, leveraging existing customer data, and using various online and offline channels to encourage sign-ups, you can create a robust and targeted list that drives engagement and conversions. Regular maintenance of your contact list ensures that it remains effective, allowing you to connect with customers who are genuinely interested in your business and ready to engage.

2.4 Setting Up Automated Messages and Quick Replies

The Role of Automation in WhatsApp Marketing

Automation plays a vital role in enhancing the efficiency and effectiveness of your WhatsApp marketing strategy. By setting up automated messages and quick replies, you can ensure timely communication with your customers, provide instant responses to common queries, and maintain a consistent brand presence, even outside of business hours. Automated messages and quick replies not only save time but also improve customer satisfaction by delivering prompt and relevant information.

Types of Automated Messages

1. Greeting Messages

Greeting messages are the first point of contact between your business and a potential customer on WhatsApp. These messages are automatically sent when a customer initiates a conversation with your business for the first time or after a period of inactivity. A well-crafted greeting message sets the tone for the interaction and makes a positive first impression.

Key Elements of a Greeting Message:

- A warm and welcoming tone that reflects your brand's personality.
- A brief introduction to your business or the specific service the customer has contacted you about.
- An invitation to ask questions or explore further, along with a mention of any available resources (like a website link or product catalog).

Example: "Hello and welcome to [Your Business Name]! We're excited to assist you. How can we help you today? Feel free to ask any questions or browse our product catalog here: [Link]."

2. Away Messages

Away messages are sent automatically when you are not available to respond immediately, such as outside of business hours or during holidays. These messages inform customers that their inquiry has been received and provide them with alternative ways to get assistance or an estimate of when they can expect a reply.

Key Elements of an Away Message:

- A polite acknowledgment of the customer's message.
- Information on your business hours or availability.
- Alternative contact options, such as an email address, website, or FAQ link.
- An estimated time when the customer can expect a response.

Example: "Thank you for reaching out to [Your Business Name]. Our team is currently unavailable, but we'll get back to you as soon as possible. Our business hours are [Insert Hours]. For urgent inquiries, please email us at [Email Address] or visit our FAQ page: [Link]."

3. Quick Replies

Quick replies are pre-written responses that can be used to answer frequently asked questions or provide common information quickly. These replies are especially useful for handling routine inquiries, such as product details, pricing, or store hours, without needing to type out a response each time. Quick replies can be accessed easily by typing a shortcut, saving time and ensuring consistency in your communication.

Key Elements of a Quick Reply:

- A clear and concise answer to the most common questions.
- Relevant details that the customer needs, such as pricing, availability, or instructions.

- A friendly tone that aligns with your brand's voice.

Example: Shortcut: "/hours" Quick Reply: "Our business hours are Monday to Friday, 9 AM to 6 PM, and Saturday, 10 AM to 4 PM. We look forward to serving you during these times!"

Setting Up Automated Messages and Quick Replies

1. Configuring Greeting Messages

To set up a greeting message in the WhatsApp Business app, follow these steps:

- Open the app and go to the Settings menu.
- Select Business Tools and then choose Greeting Message.
- Turn on the feature and customize your message. You can include text, links, or even emojis to make it more engaging.

Save your settings, and your greeting message will now be automatically sent to new or returning customers who haven't interacted with your business in a while.

2. Setting Up Away Messages

To configure away messages:

- In the Business Tools section, select Away Message.
- Turn on the away message feature and specify when it should be sent (e.g., outside of business hours or during specific times).
- Write your message, keeping it clear and informative.
- You can choose to send the away message to everyone, or only to specific contacts or new customers.
- Save your settings, and your away message will be automatically sent during the times you've specified.

3. Creating Quick Replies

To create quick replies:

- Go to the Business Tools menu and select Quick Replies.
- Tap on the + icon to create a new quick reply.
- Enter your message in the text field, and assign a shortcut (e.g., "/price" for pricing inquiries).
- Save the quick reply. Now, when you type the assigned shortcut in a chat, the pre-written message will appear, ready to send.

Best Practices for Automated Messages and Quick Replies

- **Keep It Personal**: While automation is convenient, try to maintain a personal touch in your messages. Use the customer's name whenever possible, and avoid making the messages sound overly robotic.
- **Review and Update Regularly**: As your business evolves, so will the types of inquiries you receive. Regularly review your

automated messages and quick replies to ensure they remain relevant and accurate.

- **Test Your Messages**: Before fully implementing automated messages, test them to ensure they are working correctly and are being sent at the appropriate times. This helps avoid any potential issues or misunderstandings.
- **Balance Automation with Human Interaction**: While automation is helpful, it's important to balance it with genuine human interaction. Ensure that there is always an option for customers to speak to a real person if needed.

Setting up automated messages and quick replies is a smart way to enhance your WhatsApp marketing efforts. These tools allow you to maintain a consistent, professional communication channel with your customers, even when you're not available to respond in real time. By configuring greeting messages, away messages, and quick replies effectively, you can improve customer satisfaction, save time, and focus on growing your business. Regularly updating and personalizing these messages ensures that your communication remains relevant and engaging.

Chapter 3: Crafting a WhatsApp Marketing Strategy

1. Defining Your Marketing Goals

The foundation of any successful marketing strategy begins with clearly defining your goals. In the context of WhatsApp marketing, your goals might vary depending on the nature of your business, target audience, and the specific outcomes you wish to achieve. These goals could include increasing brand awareness, driving sales, enhancing customer engagement, improving customer support, or fostering loyalty among existing customers.

When setting your marketing goals, it's crucial to ensure they are SMART: Specific, Measurable, Achievable, Relevant, and Time-bound. For example, instead of aiming to "increase customer engagement," you might set a goal to "increase the open rate of WhatsApp messages by 20% within the next three months." Having clear and actionable goals will guide your strategy and help you measure its success.

2. Identifying and Understanding Your Target Audience

Understanding your target audience is critical to crafting a WhatsApp marketing strategy that resonates with them. Begin by identifying who your ideal customers are, considering factors such as age, gender, location, interests, and purchasing behavior. This demographic and psychographic information will help you tailor your messages to meet their specific needs and preferences.

Beyond basic demographics, delve deeper into understanding the pain points and challenges your audience faces, as well as what motivates them. This insight will enable you to create content that not only captures their attention but also provides value, ultimately leading to higher engagement and conversion rates.

Conducting surveys, analyzing customer data, and monitoring social media interactions are effective ways to gather insights about your audience. Additionally, segmenting your audience based on different criteria allows you to personalize your WhatsApp marketing efforts, ensuring that each message resonates with the specific group it's intended for.

3. Developing Your Brand Voice and Messaging

Your brand voice and messaging are crucial components of your WhatsApp marketing strategy. They define how your business communicates with your audience and play a significant role in shaping your brand's identity and perception.

To develop a strong brand voice, consider the personality you want your brand to convey. Are you formal and professional, or casual and friendly? Your voice should be consistent across all communications, creating a cohesive brand experience for your customers.

When crafting your messaging, focus on delivering clear, concise, and value-driven content. WhatsApp is a personal and direct platform, so your messages should feel conversational and engaging, rather than overly promotional. Use this opportunity to build a connection with your audience by providing helpful information, answering questions, and offering personalized recommendations.

4. Planning Your Content Strategy

A well-planned content strategy is essential for keeping your WhatsApp audience engaged over time. Your content should align with your overall marketing goals and be designed to address the needs and interests of your target audience.

Start by outlining the types of content you plan to share on WhatsApp. This could include product updates, exclusive promotions, customer stories, educational tips, or behind-the-scenes glimpses of your business. Diversifying your content keeps your audience interested and ensures that your messages remain fresh and relevant.

It's also important to establish a content calendar to plan your messages. This will help you maintain consistency and ensure that you are regularly engaging with your audience. Consider the timing and frequency of your messages as well; you don't want to overwhelm your audience with too many messages, but you also don't want to go silent for too long.

5. Setting Up Metrics and KPIs

To measure the effectiveness of your WhatsApp marketing strategy, you need to establish key performance indicators (KPIs) and metrics. These metrics will help you track progress toward your goals and make data-driven decisions to optimize your strategy.

Some common KPIs for WhatsApp marketing include:

- **Open Rate**: The percentage of recipients who open your messages.
- **Click-Through Rate (CTR)**: The percentage of recipients who click on links or take action based on your messages.
- **Engagement Rate**: The level of interaction your messages receive, such as replies or shares.
- **Conversion Rate**: The percentage of recipients who complete a desired action, such as making a purchase or signing up for a service.
- **Customer Retention Rate**: The percentage of customers who continue to engage with your business over time.

By regularly monitoring these KPIs, you can identify what's working and what needs improvement. This ongoing analysis will allow you to refine your strategy, ensuring that your WhatsApp marketing efforts remain effective and aligned with your business objectives.

6. Integrating WhatsApp Marketing with Other Channels

To maximize the impact of your WhatsApp marketing strategy, it's important to integrate it with your other marketing channels. This creates a cohesive and seamless customer experience, allowing your audience to interact with your brand across multiple touchpoints.

For example, you can use email marketing to invite your subscribers to join your WhatsApp list for exclusive updates or promotions. On social media, you can promote your WhatsApp channel by sharing a direct link to your chat or showcasing the benefits of connecting with you on WhatsApp.

Additionally, consider how WhatsApp can complement your offline marketing efforts. For instance, you can encourage in-store customers to join your WhatsApp list by offering a special discount or incentive. By creating a unified marketing approach, you enhance your brand's visibility and increase the chances of engaging your audience across different platforms.

7. Adjusting and Optimizing Your Strategy

A successful WhatsApp marketing strategy is not static; it requires continuous monitoring, adjustment, and optimization. Regularly review your KPIs and metrics to assess the performance of your campaigns. If you notice that certain messages are not resonating with your audience, or if your engagement rates are declining, it's important to identify the underlying issues and make the necessary adjustments.

Experiment with different types of content, messaging styles, and timing to see what works best for your audience. A/B testing, where you compare the performance of two different versions of a message, can provide valuable insights into what drives better results.

Remember to stay updated with WhatsApp's features and best practices, as the platform continues to evolve. Adapting your strategy to take advantage of new tools or trends can give you a competitive edge and help you maintain strong connections with your audience.

Crafting a WhatsApp marketing strategy involves careful planning, thoughtful execution, and ongoing optimization. By defining clear goals, understanding your audience, developing a strong brand voice, and creating a compelling content strategy, you can build a successful WhatsApp marketing campaign that drives engagement and delivers results. Regularly monitoring your KPIs and integrating your efforts with other channels ensures that your strategy remains effective and aligned with your overall business objectives.

3.1 Defining Your Target Audience and Objectives

Understanding the Target Audience

Defining your target audience is the cornerstone of any successful marketing strategy, and WhatsApp marketing is no exception. Knowing who your audience is allows you to tailor your messages to meet their specific needs, preferences, and pain points. This personalized approach not only enhances the effectiveness of your campaigns but also fosters a deeper connection with your customers, leading to higher engagement and conversion rates.

To start, consider the demographic factors that define your audience, such as age, gender, location, and occupation. These basic characteristics give you a broad understanding of who your audience is and where they can be found. For instance, if your product is targeted at young adults, understanding their online behavior, interests, and communication preferences will help you craft messages that resonate with them.

Next, delve into psychographic details, which include your audience's values, lifestyles, and motivations. Psychographics provide deeper insights into why your audience makes decisions, what drives their behaviors, and how they perceive your brand. For example, if your target audience values sustainability, incorporating eco-friendly messaging into your WhatsApp campaigns can make your brand more appealing to them.

It's also important to segment your audience based on their behavior and engagement with your brand. Behavioral segmentation allows you to create tailored messages for different customer segments, such as new customers, repeat buyers, or inactive users. This segmentation ensures that your marketing efforts are targeted and relevant, increasing the likelihood of achieving your campaign objectives.

Defining Your Marketing Objectives

Once you have a clear understanding of your target audience, the next step is to define your marketing objectives. These objectives should align with your overall business goals and provide a clear direction for your WhatsApp marketing efforts. Establishing well-defined objectives helps you measure the success of your campaigns and make informed decisions to optimize your strategy.

When defining your objectives, it's crucial to make them SMART: Specific, Measurable, Achievable, Relevant, and Time-bound. This framework ensures that your goals are clear and actionable, providing a roadmap for your marketing activities.

- **Specific**: Clearly define what you want to achieve with your WhatsApp marketing efforts. For example, rather than setting a vague goal like "increase customer engagement," specify the exact type of engagement you're aiming for, such as "increase the response rate to customer inquiries by 30%."
- **Measurable**: Ensure that your objectives can be quantified and tracked. This allows you to monitor progress and determine whether your campaigns are successful. For instance, you might aim to "grow the number of WhatsApp subscribers by 15% in the next quarter."
- **Achievable**: Set realistic goals that are within your reach given your resources, budget, and time constraints. While ambitious goals can be motivating, setting unattainable objectives can lead to frustration and wasted effort.
- **Relevant**: Align your WhatsApp marketing objectives with your broader business goals. For example, if your company's focus is on customer retention, your WhatsApp marketing objective might be

to "reduce customer churn by 10% through personalized messaging campaigns."

- **Time-bound**: Establish a clear timeline for achieving your objectives. This creates a sense of urgency and helps you stay focused on delivering results within a specific period. For example, "increase sales by 20% through WhatsApp promotions within the next six months."

Examples of WhatsApp Marketing Objectives

To illustrate how these principles can be applied, here are some examples of WhatsApp marketing objectives:

- **Increase Brand Awareness**: Objective: "Expand brand visibility by growing our WhatsApp contact list by 25% over the next quarter through targeted social media ads and in-store promotions."
- **Drive Sales**: Objective: "Boost sales by 15% within three months by launching a series of time-limited promotional campaigns exclusively on WhatsApp."
- **Enhance Customer Support**: Objective: "Improve customer satisfaction by reducing the average response time to customer inquiries on WhatsApp from 12 hours to 3 hours within two months."
- **Foster Customer Loyalty**: Objective: "Increase repeat purchase rates by 10% in six months by implementing a personalized WhatsApp messaging campaign for loyalty program members."
- **Generate Leads**: Objective: "Generate 200 qualified leads through WhatsApp by offering a free consultation service promoted via targeted Facebook ads over the next three months."

Aligning Audience Insights with Objectives

The final step in defining your target audience and objectives is to ensure that your audience insights are aligned with your marketing goals. This alignment ensures that your campaigns are not only reaching the right people but also delivering the right messages that resonate with them.

For example, if your objective is to drive sales among young adults, your WhatsApp messages should be tailored to their preferences, such as offering trendy product recommendations or highlighting limited-time offers. Similarly, if your goal is to enhance customer support, understanding the common issues your audience faces will help you develop automated quick replies and personalized responses that address their needs promptly.

By aligning your target audience insights with your marketing objectives, you can create a WhatsApp marketing strategy that is both effective and efficient, driving meaningful results for your business.

Defining your target audience and objectives is a critical step in crafting a successful WhatsApp marketing strategy. By understanding who your audience is, what motivates them, and what they expect from your brand, you can tailor your marketing efforts to meet their needs. Clear, well-defined objectives provide direction and focus, enabling you to measure success and optimize your campaigns effectively. With these foundational elements in place, your WhatsApp marketing strategy is poised to deliver impactful results.

3.2 Content Planning: What Works Best on WhatsApp

Understanding WhatsApp's Unique Content Environment

WhatsApp is distinct from other social media platforms due to its private, direct, and personal nature. This messaging app is designed for one-on-one or small-group interactions, making it an ideal platform for personalized communication and targeted messaging. Unlike social networks where content is broadcast to a broad audience, WhatsApp content needs to be crafted with an intimate tone, fostering direct engagement with your audience.

When planning content for WhatsApp, it's essential to recognize that users value authenticity and relevance. They are more likely to engage with content that feels personal and directly applicable to their needs or interests. Given the conversational nature of the platform, content that encourages interaction and builds a relationship with your audience is most effective.

Types of Content That Work Best on WhatsApp

1. Personalized Messages

One of the most powerful aspects of WhatsApp is the ability to send personalized messages directly to your audience. Whether you're addressing customers by name or tailoring content based on their past interactions with your brand, personalized messages make your audience feel valued and understood. This could include birthday wishes with a special offer, personalized product recommendations based on previous purchases, or exclusive updates tailored to specific customer segments.

Personalized messages are particularly effective for nurturing relationships, encouraging repeat business, and enhancing customer loyalty. By leveraging customer data and behavior insights, you can create messages that resonate on a personal level, driving higher engagement and conversions.

2. Exclusive Offers and Promotions

WhatsApp is an excellent platform for delivering exclusive offers and promotions. Since the app is typically used for close contacts and trusted businesses, customers often perceive promotions received through WhatsApp as more valuable and trustworthy. This perception makes them more likely to act on the offers.

For example, you could offer limited-time discounts, early access to sales, or special deals available only to your WhatsApp subscribers. By positioning these offers as exclusive, you create a sense of urgency and privilege, encouraging immediate action from your audience.

3. Rich Media Content

Rich media content—such as images, videos, voice notes, and GIFs—enhances the engagement level of your WhatsApp messages. Visual content, in particular, is highly effective in capturing attention and conveying information quickly. For example, a short video tutorial on how to use a product, a series of images showcasing new arrivals, or a voice message from a company representative can create a more immersive and engaging experience.

Given the nature of WhatsApp, where users are often on the go, short and impactful media content tends to perform best. Ensure that your media is optimized for mobile devices and that it loads quickly, as this will enhance the user experience and increase the likelihood of engagement.

4. Educational Content and Tips

Providing valuable, educational content is a great way to position your brand as a trusted resource. On WhatsApp, you can share tips, how-to guides, or industry insights that help your audience solve problems or make informed decisions. For instance, a beauty brand might share skincare tips or a tech company could offer quick troubleshooting advice.

This type of content not only helps your audience but also builds your authority in your niche. By consistently delivering valuable information, you keep your audience engaged and encourage them to look to your brand as a go-to source for relevant expertise.

5. Customer Stories and Testimonials

Sharing customer stories and testimonials through WhatsApp can be highly effective in building trust and credibility. People tend to trust recommendations from others, so showcasing positive experiences from satisfied customers can influence potential buyers. You can share these stories in text form, or create short video testimonials for a more engaging presentation.

Moreover, customer stories can be tailored to different segments of your audience. For instance, if you're targeting small business owners, you might share a success story from another small business that benefited from your product or service.

6. Surveys and Polls

WhatsApp's interactive nature makes it a suitable platform for gathering feedback through surveys and polls. These tools allow you to engage your audience directly, gain insights into their preferences, and involve them in decision-making processes. For example, you could ask your customers to vote on a new product feature or gather feedback on a recent purchase experience.

Surveys and polls can also be used to segment your audience further, helping you tailor future communications even more precisely. Keep these interactions short and easy to complete to encourage participation.

Best Practices for Content Planning on WhatsApp

1. Keep Messages Concise

WhatsApp users value brevity. Messages should be concise, clear, and to the point. Avoid long blocks of text that may overwhelm the reader. Instead, break up your content into digestible chunks, and use paragraphs, bullet points, or headings to make it easier to scan.

2. Use Call-to-Actions (CTAs)

Every piece of content you share on WhatsApp should have a clear call-to-action (CTA). Whether it's prompting users to visit your website, make a purchase, participate in a survey, or simply reply to your message, a strong CTA guides the recipient toward the desired outcome.

Make sure your CTA is specific and aligned with the goal of your message.

3. Maintain a Consistent Schedule

Consistency is key to keeping your audience engaged. Plan a regular schedule for your WhatsApp messages, whether it's daily tips, weekly updates, or monthly promotions. However, be mindful not to overwhelm your audience with too frequent messages. Striking the right balance between staying top of mind and respecting your audience's time is crucial.

4. Encourage Two-Way Communication

WhatsApp is inherently a conversational platform, so encourage two-way communication with your audience. Prompt responses, ask questions and invite feedback. Engaging in dialogues with your customers helps build stronger relationships and provides valuable insights into their needs and preferences.

5. Monitor and Adjust Content Based on Performance

Regularly review the performance of your WhatsApp content. Pay attention to metrics like open rates, response rates, and conversion rates to understand what works best with your audience. Use these insights to refine your content strategy, ensuring that you continuously deliver value and relevance.

Content planning for WhatsApp requires a thoughtful approach that leverages the platform's unique strengths—personalization, directness, and engagement. By focusing on personalized messages, exclusive offers, rich media, educational content, customer stories, and interactive polls, you can create a compelling WhatsApp marketing strategy that resonates with your audience. Following best practices such as keeping messages concise, using clear CTAs, maintaining consistency, encouraging two-way communication, and regularly adjusting your strategy will ensure that your WhatsApp marketing efforts are both effective and impactful.

3.3 Integrating WhatsApp with Your Overall Marketing Strategy

The Importance of Integration

Integrating WhatsApp into your overall marketing strategy is essential for creating a cohesive and unified brand experience across all customer touchpoints. WhatsApp, with its highly personal and direct communication style, can complement your existing marketing channels and enhance the effectiveness of your campaigns. When integrated seamlessly, WhatsApp can drive higher engagement, foster deeper customer relationships, and ultimately contribute to achieving your broader marketing goals.

Integration also ensures that your messaging remains consistent across platforms, reinforcing your brand identity and values. Whether your audience interacts with you on social media, via email, or through WhatsApp, they should encounter a consistent voice, style, and message. This consistency builds trust and makes your brand more recognizable and reliable in the eyes of your customers.

Aligning WhatsApp with Other Marketing Channels

1. Social Media Integration

Social media platforms like Facebook, Instagram, and Twitter are often the first point of contact between a brand and its audience. By integrating WhatsApp into your social media strategy, you can create a more direct line of communication with your followers, converting casual interactions into meaningful engagements.

For example, you can promote your WhatsApp number or link through your social media profiles and posts, inviting followers to connect with you for exclusive offers, customer support, or personalized content. Facebook, which owns WhatsApp, even allows you to add a WhatsApp button to your business page, making it easier for users to reach you directly from your Facebook page.

Moreover, social media can be used to drive traffic to your WhatsApp channel. Running targeted ads that encourage users to message your business on WhatsApp can help you grow your contact list and engage with potential customers in a more intimate setting. These ads can offer incentives, such as a discount code or access to premium content, for users who initiate a conversation on WhatsApp.

2. Email Marketing Integration

Email marketing remains one of the most effective tools for nurturing leads and maintaining customer relationships. By integrating WhatsApp with your email marketing efforts, you can create a multi-channel communication strategy that maximizes reach and engagement.

One way to integrate these channels is by using email to promote your WhatsApp channel. For instance, you can include a call-to-action (CTA) in your emails, inviting subscribers to join your WhatsApp list for more immediate updates, special offers, or customer support. This approach not only diversifies your communication channels but also allows you to reach customers in the medium they prefer.

Conversely, you can use WhatsApp to complement your email campaigns by sending reminders or follow-up messages. If you've sent out a promotional email, a quick WhatsApp message reminding subscribers about the offer can increase conversion rates. This type of cross-channel promotion ensures that your message reaches your audience through multiple touchpoints, reinforcing your marketing efforts.

3. Website Integration

Your website is the digital home of your brand, where customers come to learn more about your products, services, and values. Integrating WhatsApp with your website can enhance the user experience by providing a quick and convenient way for visitors to get in touch with you.

One of the most effective ways to integrate WhatsApp with your website is by adding a WhatsApp chat button or widget. This allows visitors to start a conversation with your business with a single click, whether they need customer support, have a question about a product, or are interested in making a purchase. A WhatsApp chat button can be strategically placed on key pages of your website, such as the homepage, product pages, or checkout page, to encourage interaction at critical points in the customer journey.

You can also use WhatsApp to deliver personalized content directly to your website visitors. For example, if a visitor has abandoned their shopping cart, you can send a personalized message via WhatsApp with a gentle reminder or an exclusive discount to encourage them to complete their purchase. This type of real-time engagement can significantly improve conversion rates and enhance customer satisfaction.

4. Content Marketing Integration

Content marketing is all about providing valuable, relevant content to attract and retain your target audience. WhatsApp can be a powerful distribution channel for your content, allowing you to reach your audience with tailored messages that complement your broader content strategy.

For instance, you can share blog posts, videos, or infographics via WhatsApp to provide your audience with educational content, tips, and insights that align with their interests. This not only adds value to their experience but also drives traffic back to your website or other content platforms.

Additionally, WhatsApp can be used to deliver exclusive content that's not available on other channels. For example, you can create a VIP list of subscribers who receive early access to new blog posts, e-books, or webinars. This approach not only rewards your most engaged followers but also encourages others to join your WhatsApp list to gain access to premium content.

Creating a Seamless Customer Journey

A key aspect of integrating WhatsApp with your overall marketing strategy is ensuring a seamless customer journey across all touchpoints. Your customers should be able to move effortlessly between channels, receiving a consistent and unified experience at every stage.

For example, a customer might discover your brand through a social media ad, visit your website to learn more, sign up for your email newsletter, and then receive a personalized message on WhatsApp offering a special discount on their first purchase. Each interaction should feel connected and purposeful, guiding the customer through the sales funnel without friction.

To create this seamless experience, it's important to map out the customer journey and identify key touchpoints where WhatsApp can add value. By understanding how your audience interacts with your brand across different channels, you can strategically incorporate WhatsApp into the journey, ensuring that it enhances rather than disrupts the overall experience.

Tracking and Measuring Integration Success

To ensure that your integration efforts are effective, it's important to track and measure key performance indicators (KPIs) across all channels. This will help you assess how well WhatsApp is contributing to your overall marketing goals and identify areas for improvement.

Some KPIs to monitor include:

- **Engagement Rates**: Track how many people are interacting with your WhatsApp messages compared to other channels.
- **Conversion Rates**: Measure the impact of WhatsApp on driving sales, sign-ups, or other desired actions.
- **Customer Retention**: Assess how WhatsApp contributes to customer loyalty and repeat business.
- **Cross-Channel Traffic**: Monitor how effectively WhatsApp drives traffic to your website, social media profiles, or other platforms.

By regularly reviewing these metrics, you can optimize your strategy and ensure that WhatsApp is fully integrated into your marketing efforts, driving the best possible results for your business.

Integrating WhatsApp with your overall marketing strategy is crucial for creating a cohesive, multi-channel approach that maximizes customer engagement and drives meaningful results. By aligning WhatsApp with your social media, email marketing, website, and content marketing efforts, you can create a seamless customer journey that enhances the overall brand experience. Regularly tracking and measuring your integration success will ensure that WhatsApp continues to play a valuable role in your marketing strategy, helping you achieve your business objectives.

3.4 Legal and Ethical Considerations

Understanding the Regulatory Landscape

As with any form of digital marketing, WhatsApp marketing is subject to various legal and ethical guidelines designed to protect consumer rights and privacy. These regulations differ by region and can have significant implications for how you use WhatsApp to engage with your audience. It's essential to familiarize yourself with the relevant laws to ensure your marketing practices are compliant and respectful of your customers' rights.

In many regions, laws such as the General Data Protection Regulation (GDPR) in the European Union, the California Consumer Privacy Act (CCPA) in the United States, and other data protection regulations govern how businesses can collect, store, and use personal data. These laws mandate that businesses obtain explicit consent from individuals before using their personal information for marketing purposes and that they provide clear options for opting out of communications.

Failure to comply with these regulations can result in significant penalties, damage to your brand's reputation, and a loss of customer trust. Therefore, understanding the legal requirements in your operating regions is crucial for implementing a successful and compliant WhatsApp marketing strategy.

Obtaining Consent

One of the fundamental principles of ethical WhatsApp marketing is obtaining consent from your audience before sending them messages. This consent should be informed, meaning that your customers are fully aware of what they are signing up for and how their data will be used. Consent is not just a legal requirement; it's also an ethical obligation that demonstrates respect for your customers' privacy and autonomy.

When collecting phone numbers for your WhatsApp marketing campaigns, it's essential to be transparent about how you intend to use them. This can be done by providing clear, concise information at the point of collection, such as on your website, social media channels, or in physical stores. You should also give customers the option to opt in or out of receiving WhatsApp messages, ensuring that their participation is voluntary.

For example, if you're asking customers to sign up for updates via WhatsApp, make it clear what types of messages they can expect (e.g., promotions, news, customer support) and how often they will receive them. You might also include a link to your privacy policy, where customers can find more detailed information about how their data will be handled.

In addition to obtaining initial consent, it's important to regularly review and renew consent, especially if your marketing practices change or if there are significant updates to your privacy policy. Providing an easy way for customers to opt out of WhatsApp communications at any time is also essential for maintaining trust and compliance.

Respecting Customer Privacy

Privacy is a critical concern for consumers, especially in an era where data breaches and misuse of personal information are increasingly common. When using WhatsApp for marketing, it's essential to prioritize customer privacy and take all necessary steps to protect their data.

Firstly, ensure that any personal information you collect and store is secured against unauthorized access. This includes using encryption, secure servers, and other cybersecurity measures to protect data from breaches. WhatsApp itself uses end-to-end encryption for all messages, which adds a layer of security, but it's still your responsibility to safeguard customer data on your end.

Secondly, be mindful of the type of content you share and the frequency of your messages. Avoid overloading your customers with excessive communications, as this can be perceived as intrusive and may lead to them blocking your number or unsubscribing from your messages. Instead, focus on delivering value with each message, ensuring that your content is relevant and respectful of your customers' time and attention.

It's also important to avoid sharing sensitive information through WhatsApp, such as financial details or personal identification numbers. If you need to handle such information, consider using a more secure channel or ensuring that both parties understand the risks and agree to proceed with caution.

Managing Data Responsibly

Data management is a key component of legal and ethical WhatsApp marketing. This involves not only collecting and storing data securely but also using it responsibly and transparently. As a marketer, you must handle customer data in a way that respects their privacy and adheres to relevant legal standards.

One important aspect of responsible data management is data minimization, which means collecting only the data you need for specific, legitimate purposes. Avoid gathering unnecessary or excessive information, as this can increase the risk of data breaches and may lead to non-compliance with data protection laws.

Additionally, ensure that you have clear policies in place for how data will be used, stored, and eventually deleted. For example, if a customer decides to opt out of your WhatsApp marketing communications, their data should be promptly removed from your marketing lists. Regularly auditing your data practices can help ensure that you remain compliant with legal requirements and that you continue to uphold high ethical standards.

Transparency is also crucial when it comes to data management. Customers should be able to easily access information about what data you have collected, how it's being used, and how they can manage or delete their information. Providing clear instructions and accessible support channels for these purposes is an essential part of maintaining trust and compliance.

Avoiding Spam and Misleading Practices

One of the most common ethical pitfalls in digital marketing is the use of spammy or misleading practices to engage customers. WhatsApp's personal and direct nature makes it particularly important to avoid these tactics, as they can quickly erode trust and damage your brand's reputation.

Spam is any unsolicited or irrelevant messaging that clutters your customers' inboxes and detracts from their experience. To avoid spamming your audience, ensure that your messages are always relevant, personalized, and valuable. Sending too many messages, especially those that are repetitive or not aligned with the customer's interests, can lead to frustration and prompt users to block your number.

Similarly, it's important to be honest and transparent in your communications. Avoid making exaggerated claims or misleading statements that could deceive your audience. For example, if you're promoting a limited-time offer, make sure that the terms and conditions are clear and accurate, and that the offer is genuinely time-sensitive.

Ethical marketing also means being respectful of cultural and social sensitivities. Be mindful of the language and imagery you use, and avoid content that could be considered offensive or inappropriate for your audience. This consideration is especially important when marketing to a global audience, as cultural norms and expectations can vary widely across different regions.

Complying with WhatsApp's Business Policy

In addition to adhering to legal and ethical guidelines, it's important to comply with WhatsApp's business policy. WhatsApp has strict rules about how businesses can use the platform, including restrictions on certain types of content and practices. Non-compliance with these rules can result in your account being banned or restricted, so it's essential to familiarize yourself with WhatsApp's guidelines.

Key points from WhatsApp's business policy include:

- **No Unauthorized Bulk Messaging**: WhatsApp prohibits the use of the platform for unauthorized bulk messaging, automated messaging, or spamming. Ensure that all messages sent through WhatsApp are targeted, relevant, and consented to by the recipient.
- **Respectful Content**: WhatsApp requires that all content shared on the platform is respectful and complies with local laws. Avoid sharing content that is illegal, offensive, or otherwise inappropriate.
- **Transparency with Customers**: WhatsApp encourages businesses to be transparent with their customers about how they use the platform and to provide clear ways for customers to manage their interactions with the business.

By adhering to WhatsApp's policies, you can ensure that your marketing efforts are not only effective but also sustainable and in line with the platform's expectations.

Legal and ethical considerations are integral to a successful WhatsApp marketing strategy. By understanding the regulatory landscape, obtaining proper consent, respecting customer privacy, managing data responsibly, and avoiding spammy or misleading practices, you can build a compliant and trustworthy marketing approach. Moreover, aligning your practices with WhatsApp's business policy ensures that your efforts are sustainable and well-received by both your audience and the platform itself. By prioritizing ethics and legality in your WhatsApp marketing, you not only protect your business from potential risks but also foster stronger, more respectful relationships with your customers.

Chapter 4: Building and Nurturing Your WhatsApp Audience

Building and nurturing a WhatsApp audience is a critical component of any successful WhatsApp marketing strategy. Unlike other platforms, WhatsApp allows for direct, personalized communication with your audience, which can lead to stronger relationships and higher engagement rates. However, to fully leverage the platform's potential, it's essential to focus not only on growing your contact list but also on nurturing those relationships over time.

This chapter will guide you through the process of building a robust WhatsApp audience and provide strategies for keeping that audience engaged and loyal to your brand. By focusing on both acquisition and retention, you'll be able to maximize the impact of your WhatsApp marketing efforts.

1. Growing Your WhatsApp Audience: Strategies for Success

Growing your WhatsApp audience starts with attracting the right people to your contact list. This involves using various channels and tactics to reach potential customers and encouraging them to connect with you on WhatsApp.

Leverage Existing Channels

Your existing marketing channels, such as social media, email newsletters, and your website, are valuable tools for promoting your WhatsApp number or link. For example, you can include a call-to-action in your email campaigns inviting subscribers to join your WhatsApp list for exclusive updates or special offers. Similarly, adding a WhatsApp button or widget to your website can make it easy for visitors to start a conversation with you.

Offer Incentives

Incentives are a powerful way to encourage people to sign up for your WhatsApp communications. Offering discounts, freebies, or access to exclusive content can motivate potential customers to join your list. Make sure the incentive is relevant and valuable to your target audience, and communicate the benefits of connecting with you on WhatsApp.

Run Targeted Ads

If you want to accelerate your audience growth, consider running targeted ads on platforms like Facebook and Instagram that drive users to your WhatsApp number. These ads can be highly effective, especially if they are targeted to specific demographics or interests that align with your ideal customer profile. Be sure to craft compelling ad copy and visuals that highlight the benefits of joining your WhatsApp list.

Collaborate with Influencers

Influencers who resonate with your target audience can help promote your WhatsApp channel. Partnering with influencers to create content or run campaigns that encourage their followers to connect with your brand on WhatsApp can be a highly effective way to grow your audience. Make sure to choose influencers whose values align with your brand and whose audience is likely to be interested in your products or services.

2. Engaging Your Audience: Strategies for Building Relationships

Once you've built a strong WhatsApp audience, the next step is to keep them engaged. Engagement is key to maintaining customer interest and fostering long-term relationships. This section will explore various strategies for keeping your audience actively involved with your brand on WhatsApp.

Personalized Communication

Personalization is one of the biggest advantages of WhatsApp marketing. Unlike other platforms where messages are often broadcast to a broad audience, WhatsApp allows for one-on-one communication. Take advantage of this by personalizing your messages based on customer preferences, behaviors, and interactions with your brand. Whether it's addressing customers by name, tailoring content to their interests, or sending personalized offers, these efforts can significantly enhance engagement.

Timely and Relevant Content

Timing is crucial in WhatsApp marketing. Sending messages at the right time can increase the likelihood of them being read and acted upon. Pay attention to when your audience is most active and schedule your messages accordingly. Additionally, ensure that your content is relevant to your audience's current needs and interests. For instance, if you're running a seasonal promotion, tailor your messages to reflect the season's themes and trends.

Interactive Content

Interactive content can significantly boost engagement on WhatsApp. Polls, quizzes, and contests are great ways to get your audience involved and encourage them to interact with your brand. For example, you could run a quiz related to your products or services, with a discount or prize for those who participate. Interactive content not only entertains your audience but also provides valuable insights into their preferences and behaviors.

Exclusive Offers and Updates

One of the best ways to keep your WhatsApp audience engaged is by offering them something they can't get elsewhere. Exclusive offers, early access to new products, or insider updates can make your audience feel valued and appreciated. This exclusivity can encourage them to stay subscribed to your WhatsApp communications and engage more regularly with your brand.

3. Retaining Your Audience: Strategies for Long-Term Loyalty

Retaining your WhatsApp audience is just as important as acquiring them. Loyalty is built over time through consistent, value-driven communication that meets your audience's needs. In this section, we'll explore strategies for maintaining long-term relationships with your WhatsApp audience.

Consistent Communication

Consistency is key to keeping your audience engaged over the long term. Regular communication helps keep your brand top-of-mind and reinforces the relationship you've built with your audience. However, it's important to strike a balance between staying in touch and overwhelming your audience with too many messages. Establish a regular communication schedule that provides value without being intrusive.

Customer Feedback and Involvement

Encouraging customer feedback is an effective way to keep your audience engaged and involved in your brand. Use WhatsApp to ask for opinions, suggestions, or reviews, and show your audience that you value their input. Involving them in decision-making processes, such as product development or content creation, can also foster a sense of community and loyalty.

Provide Exceptional Customer Support

WhatsApp is an ideal platform for providing quick, personalized customer support. Offering responsive and helpful support can greatly enhance customer satisfaction and loyalty. Ensure that your support team is well-trained in handling inquiries and issues on WhatsApp, and strive to resolve problems promptly and efficiently. Going the extra mile to assist your customers can leave a lasting positive impression.

Exclusive Loyalty Programs

Consider creating a loyalty program exclusively for your WhatsApp audience. This could include rewards for frequent purchases, referrals, or engagement with your content. By offering special perks to your most loyal customers, you can incentivize continued interaction with your brand and strengthen their long-term commitment.

Building and nurturing your WhatsApp audience is a dynamic process that requires a thoughtful approach to both acquisition and retention. By growing your audience through strategic promotion and offering valuable, personalized content, you can create a loyal and engaged customer base. Maintaining this relationship through consistent communication, customer involvement, and exceptional support will help ensure long-term success for your WhatsApp marketing efforts. In the next chapter, we will explore advanced techniques for leveraging WhatsApp to drive sales and achieve your business goals.

4.1 Strategies for Growing Your Subscriber Base

Growing your WhatsApp subscriber base is the foundation of a successful WhatsApp marketing strategy. A larger and more engaged audience not only increases the potential reach of your campaigns but also provides a more substantial pool of data to refine your marketing efforts. In this section, we'll explore various strategies for effectively growing your WhatsApp subscriber base, ensuring that your efforts attract the right audience for your brand.

Optimize Your Website and Social Media Channels

Your website and social media channels are prime locations for promoting your WhatsApp number or click-to-chat link. By integrating WhatsApp into your online presence, you can make it easy for visitors and followers to connect with you.

On your website, consider placing a prominent WhatsApp button or widget on high-traffic pages, such as your homepage, product page, or contact page. Ensure that the button is visible and clearly labeled, so visitors understand they can reach you via WhatsApp. Additionally, adding a call-to-action (CTA) encouraging visitors to join your WhatsApp list for updates, special offers, or customer support can increase sign-ups.

For social media channels like Facebook, Instagram, and LinkedIn, include your WhatsApp link in your bio or as part of your post captions. Regularly remind your followers of the benefits of connecting with you on WhatsApp, such as receiving exclusive content, personalized updates, or faster customer service. The more integrated WhatsApp is with your existing online presence, the more likely users are to subscribe.

Incentivize Subscriptions

Offering incentives is a proven way to encourage users to subscribe to your WhatsApp communications. People are more likely to join your list if there's a clear, immediate benefit to them. These incentives can take various forms, depending on your business model and target audience.

Discounts or promotional offers are among the most effective incentives. For example, you could offer a percentage off their next purchase, a free product, or a special deal available only to WhatsApp subscribers. Communicate this offer on your website, social media channels, and any other marketing materials. Ensure that the process of subscribing is straightforward and that users can quickly redeem their incentive once they've joined.

Exclusive content is another powerful incentive. If your business creates valuable content, such as guides, tutorials, or industry insights, offering access to this content via WhatsApp can be a significant draw. Position this content as a premium offering available only to those who subscribe, enhancing its perceived value.

Leverage Email Marketing

Email marketing is a valuable tool for growing your WhatsApp subscriber base. If you already have an email list, you can use it to promote your WhatsApp channel and encourage subscribers to join.

Create an email campaign specifically designed to introduce your audience to your WhatsApp presence. Highlight the unique benefits of subscribing, such as instant updates, personalized messages, or exclusive offers. Include a clear CTA with a direct link to join your WhatsApp list. Consider segmenting your email list to target the most engaged subscribers first, as they are more likely to be receptive to this new channel.

Additionally, you can include a WhatsApp sign-up prompt in your regular email newsletters. A simple CTA in the email footer, inviting readers to connect on WhatsApp for more personalized communication, can gradually grow your subscriber base over time.

Run Paid Advertising Campaigns

Paid advertising on platforms like Facebook and Instagram can be a highly effective way to drive traffic to your WhatsApp number. These platforms offer sophisticated targeting options, allowing you to reach users who are most likely to be interested in your brand.

When creating ads, focus on the value proposition of joining your WhatsApp list. Use eye-catching visuals and compelling copy that communicate the benefits of subscribing. Whether you're offering exclusive deals, personalized updates, or superior customer support, make sure your ad highlights these advantages.

Consider using Facebook's "Click to WhatsApp" ads, which allow users to initiate a conversation with your business directly from the ad. This seamless integration between the ad and WhatsApp makes it easy for users to connect, increasing the likelihood of conversion. Monitor the performance of your ads closely and adjust targeting, creative, and messaging as needed to optimize results.

Partner with Influencers

Influencer marketing can be a powerful tool for growing your WhatsApp subscriber base, especially if you're targeting a specific niche or demographic. Partnering with influencers who have a strong connection with your target audience can lend credibility to your WhatsApp channel and attract new subscribers.

When working with influencers, consider creating a campaign that highlights the benefits of joining your WhatsApp list. This could involve the influencer promoting your WhatsApp number in their content, such as Instagram stories, YouTube videos, or blog posts. The influencer can share their own positive experiences with your brand on WhatsApp, encouraging their followers to subscribe.

To maximize the impact of the campaign, provide the influencer with an exclusive offer or piece of content that they can share with their audience. This not only incentivizes followers to join but also strengthens the influencer's endorsement of your brand.

Use Offline Promotion

While digital channels are crucial for growing your WhatsApp subscriber base, offline promotion should not be overlooked, especially if you have a physical presence or attend events.

In your physical stores, consider placing signage or flyers that promote your WhatsApp number. Use clear, eye-catching designs and include a strong CTA that encourages customers to subscribe for special offers, updates, or customer support. You could also include a QR code that customers can scan to join your WhatsApp list instantly.

If you attend trade shows, conferences, or other events, use these opportunities to promote your WhatsApp channel. Distribute promotional materials that include your WhatsApp number and explain the benefits of subscribing. Consider offering an event-specific incentive, such as a discount or freebie, to encourage sign-ups on the spot.

Implement Referral Programs

Referral programs can be a highly effective way to grow your WhatsApp subscriber base by leveraging your existing audience. When your current subscribers refer new users to your WhatsApp channel, it not only expands your reach but also brings in potential customers who are likely to be interested in your brand.

To implement a referral program, offer an incentive to both the referrer and the new subscriber. For example, you could provide a discount, free product, or exclusive content to the current subscriber when they successfully refer a friend. Similarly, offer a welcome incentive to the new subscribers to encourage them to stay engaged with your WhatsApp communications.

Promote your referral program through your existing WhatsApp messages, email newsletters, social media channels, and website. Make the referral process as simple as possible, and provide clear instructions on how subscribers can participate and claim their rewards.

Growing your WhatsApp subscriber base requires a multi-faceted approach that leverages both online and offline channels. By optimizing your website and social media presence, offering attractive incentives, running targeted ads, partnering with influencers, and implementing referral programs, you can attract a large and engaged audience. Remember, the quality of your subscribers is just as important as the quantity—focus on attracting individuals who are genuinely interested in your brand and who are likely to engage with your content over the long term. In the following sections, we'll discuss strategies for nurturing these subscribers and keeping them engaged with your brand.

4.2 Personalization Techniques: Engaging with Customers

Personalization is a cornerstone of successful WhatsApp marketing. Unlike more traditional marketing channels, WhatsApp allows for direct, one-on-one communication with your customers. This unique feature provides an opportunity to tailor your messages to individual preferences, behaviors, and needs, leading to deeper engagement and stronger relationships. In this section, we'll explore various personalization techniques that can enhance your WhatsApp marketing efforts and keep your customers engaged.

Segmenting Your Audience

Effective personalization begins with understanding your audience. Segmentation involves dividing your audience into distinct groups based on specific criteria, such as demographics, purchase history, behavior, or interests. By segmenting your audience, you can send targeted messages that are more relevant to each group, increasing the likelihood of engagement.

For example, if you run an online store, you might segment your audience based on their past purchases. Customers who have previously bought fitness products could receive personalized messages about new workout gear or exclusive discounts on supplements. Similarly, new subscribers could receive a welcome series that introduces them to your brand and products, while long-term customers might receive loyalty rewards or exclusive offers.

Segmentation can also be based on engagement levels. For instance, you can identify highly engaged customers and reward them with special offers, while re-engagement campaigns can be designed for those who have been inactive for a while. The key is to ensure that your messaging is tailored to the specific interests and behaviors of each segment, making your communication more relevant and effective.

Using Customer Data for Personalization

To effectively personalize your messages, you need to gather and analyze customer data. WhatsApp allows you to collect valuable data points, such as customer names, purchase history, preferences, and interaction history. By leveraging this data, you can create personalized messages that resonate with each customer.

Start by addressing customers by their names. This simple personalization technique can make your messages feel more personal and less like a generic broadcast. For example, instead of sending a message that says, "Check out our new products," a personalized message might read, "Hi [Customer Name], we thought you'd love our latest collection based on your recent purchases."

You can also use customer data to recommend products or services that are likely to interest them. For instance, if a customer frequently purchases skincare products, you could send them a personalized message about a new skincare line that matches their preferences. Additionally, you can use data on past interactions to tailor follow-up messages, such as sending a thank-you note after a purchase or offering assistance if a customer has previously inquired about a product.

Timing Your Messages for Maximum Impact

Timing plays a crucial role in the effectiveness of personalized messages. Sending messages at the right time can significantly increase open rates and engagement. WhatsApp allows you to schedule messages, ensuring that they reach your customers when they are most likely to be receptive.

To determine the best time to send messages, consider the behavior patterns of your audience. For example, if your customers tend to shop in the evenings, schedule your promotional messages to go out during that time. Similarly, if you're targeting busy professionals, sending messages during lunch breaks or after work hours might yield better results.

You can also use timing to create a sense of urgency. For instance, sending a personalized message that highlights a limited-time offer or an expiring discount can prompt customers to take immediate action. However, be mindful of not overusing this tactic, as it can lead to message fatigue if done too frequently.

Creating Customized Content

Customized content goes beyond simply personalizing messages with names or product recommendations. It involves creating content that speaks directly to the needs, interests, and preferences of each customer segment. This approach can significantly enhance engagement by making your communications more relevant and valuable.

One way to create customized content is by developing content themes based on your audience segments. For example, if you have a segment of customers interested in sustainable living, you could create content around eco-friendly products, tips for reducing waste, or information on your brand's sustainability practices. Similarly, you could develop content that aligns with specific customer journeys, such as tips for first-time buyers, care instructions for repeat customers, or inspiration for those looking to explore new product categories.

In addition to written content, consider using rich media, such as images, videos, and voice messages, to personalize your communication further. For example, you could send a personalized video message to welcome new subscribers, showcase a product in action, or provide a step-by-step tutorial. Rich media can make your content more engaging and memorable, helping to build a stronger connection with your audience.

Leveraging Automated Messaging with a Personal Touch

Automated messaging is a powerful tool for maintaining consistent communication with your audience, but it's important to balance automation with personalization to avoid coming across as impersonal or robotic. WhatsApp allows you to set up automated messages, such as welcome messages, order confirmations, or reminders, which can be personalized to enhance the customer experience.

When setting up automated messages, ensure that they include personalized elements, such as the customer's name, order details, or specific recommendations. For example, instead of a generic order confirmation message, you could send a personalized message that thanks the customer by name, provides details of their purchase, and suggests complementary products they might be interested in.

Automated messaging can also be used for follow-ups and re-engagement. For instance, if a customer hasn't interacted with your brand in a while, you could send an automated message offering a special discount to entice them back. Similarly, after a purchase, you could set up an automated message that asks for feedback, offers support, or provides tips on how to use the product effectively.

Engaging in Two-Way Conversations

One of the most powerful aspects of WhatsApp is its ability to facilitate two-way conversations. Unlike traditional marketing channels, WhatsApp allows for real-time, interactive communication with your customers. This interaction can be a key differentiator in your marketing strategy, enabling you to build stronger relationships through personalized, responsive communication.

Encourage your customers to engage with you by asking questions, soliciting feedback, or inviting them to share their thoughts. For example, after sending a promotional message, you could follow up with a question asking if they found the offer relevant or if there's anything else they're interested in. This approach not only helps you gather valuable insights but also shows your customers that you value their opinions.

When customers reach out to you, respond promptly and personalize your replies based on their inquiries. For instance, if a customer asks about product availability, respond with personalized suggestions based on their previous purchases or preferences. The key is to make every interaction feel personal and tailored to the individual, fostering a sense of connection and loyalty.

Personalization is at the heart of effective WhatsApp marketing. By segmenting your audience, leveraging customer data, timing your messages strategically, creating customized content, and balancing automation with a personal touch, you can engage your customers in meaningful ways. Additionally, fostering two-way conversations can help you build stronger, more loyal relationships with your audience. In the next section, we'll explore advanced techniques for driving sales and conversions through your personalized WhatsApp marketing efforts.

4.3 Using WhatsApp Groups and Broadcasts Effectively

WhatsApp groups and broadcasts are powerful tools that can enhance your marketing efforts, allowing you to reach multiple customers simultaneously while maintaining a degree of personalization. Understanding how to use these features effectively can help you build community, drive engagement, and streamline communication. This section will explore the strategic use of WhatsApp groups and broadcasts to maximize their potential for your business.

Harnessing the Power of WhatsApp Groups

WhatsApp groups offer a dynamic way to foster community and engage with a segmented audience. Creating groups around specific interests, topics, or customer segments can provide a more interactive and personalized experience for your audience.

To leverage WhatsApp groups effectively, start by defining the purpose of each group. Groups can be used for various purposes, such as offering customer support, sharing exclusive content, or facilitating discussions among like-minded individuals. For example, you might create a group for loyal customers where you share early access to new products, provide behind-the-scenes content, or host Q&A sessions. This not only creates a sense of exclusivity but also encourages more active participation.

Managing a WhatsApp group requires attention to ensure that it remains focused and valuable for its members. Establish clear guidelines for participation to maintain a positive and relevant environment. Encourage interaction by regularly posting engaging content, initiating discussions, and responding to members' queries. This active engagement helps build a stronger community and fosters a sense of belonging among group members.

Moreover, groups can be used for market research and feedback collection. By creating a group of engaged customers, you can directly gather insights on product preferences, campaign effectiveness, or service improvements. Use polls or surveys within the group to obtain valuable opinions and feedback that can inform your business decisions.

Utilizing WhatsApp Broadcasts for Targeted Messaging

WhatsApp broadcasts enable you to send messages to multiple recipients at once without them seeing each other's responses. This feature is particularly useful for delivering targeted updates, promotions, and announcements to a broader audience while maintaining a level of privacy and personalization.

To use broadcasts effectively, segment your contact list based on various criteria, such as demographics, purchase history, or engagement levels. This segmentation allows you to tailor your messages to specific groups, making them more relevant and engaging. For example, you might send a broadcast message about a seasonal sale to customers who have previously shown interest in related products.

Craft your broadcast messages to be concise and compelling, with a clear call to action. Since broadcast messages are sent individually to each recipient, ensure that they are personalized where possible. For instance, include the recipient's name or reference their past interactions with your brand to make the message feel more personalized.

Timing is also crucial for broadcast messages. Schedule your broadcasts to reach your audience at times when they are most likely to be receptive. Avoid sending messages too frequently, as this can lead to message fatigue and unsubscribes. Instead, focus on sending high-value content that provides real benefits to your recipients.

Balancing Privacy and Engagement

One of the key considerations when using WhatsApp groups and broadcasts is balancing privacy with engagement. Groups can foster a sense of community, but they require careful management to ensure that privacy is respected and that the conversation remains relevant to all members.

In groups, make sure to set privacy settings that align with your goals. For instance, you might choose to make groups private to prevent unwanted participants or limit group membership to those who meet certain criteria. Additionally, communicate the purpose and rules of the group to new members to set expectations and maintain a positive environment.

For broadcasts, ensure that your messages are sent only to recipients who have opted in to receive communications from you. This approach not only respects their privacy but also helps maintain a high level of engagement. Regularly review your broadcast lists and remove inactive or unengaged contacts to ensure that your messages reach a receptive audience.

Integrating Groups and Broadcasts into Your Marketing Strategy

Effectively integrating WhatsApp groups and broadcasts into your broader marketing strategy can enhance your overall communication efforts. Consider how these tools can complement your existing channels and contribute to your marketing goals.

For example, use groups as a platform for nurturing relationships with your most loyal customers, while broadcasts can be used for reaching a wider audience with targeted promotions and updates. Create a cohesive strategy that leverages the strengths of each tool to achieve your marketing objectives. Regularly analyze the performance of your groups and broadcasts to assess their impact and make adjustments as needed.

Additionally, use data from your groups and broadcasts to inform your overall marketing strategy. Track engagement metrics, such as response rates, participation levels, and feedback, to gauge the effectiveness of your communications. This data can provide valuable insights into what resonates with your audience and help you refine your messaging and tactics.

WhatsApp groups and broadcasts offer distinct advantages for engaging with your audience and delivering targeted communication. By using groups to build community and foster interaction, and leveraging broadcasts for personalized, large-scale messaging, you can enhance your marketing efforts and strengthen your relationships with customers. Balancing privacy with engagement, integrating these tools into your broader strategy, and continuously analyzing performance will help you maximize their potential and achieve your marketing goals. In the next section, we will explore advanced strategies for measuring and optimizing the impact of your WhatsApp marketing campaigns.

4.4 Handling Customer Inquiries and Feedback

Effective handling of customer inquiries and feedback is crucial for maintaining a positive brand reputation and fostering customer loyalty on WhatsApp. As a direct communication channel, WhatsApp offers a unique opportunity to engage with customers in real time, addressing their needs and concerns promptly. This section will explore best practices for managing customer interactions on WhatsApp, ensuring that inquiries and feedback are handled efficiently and professionally.

Responding to Inquiries Promptly

Timely responses to customer inquiries are essential for providing excellent customer service and demonstrating that you value your customers' time. WhatsApp's real-time messaging capability allows for immediate interaction, making it crucial to address inquiries as quickly as possible.

To ensure prompt responses, consider setting up a system for monitoring and managing incoming messages. Assign dedicated team members or use automated tools to track and respond to inquiries efficiently. Establishing response time benchmarks can help maintain consistency in service quality. For instance, aiming to respond to inquiries within 24 hours can help manage customer expectations and enhance satisfaction.

Additionally, use WhatsApp's features to streamline responses. Predefined quick replies can help address common questions and provide instant answers, reducing response time and workload. For more complex inquiries, ensure that responses are thoughtful and detailed, addressing the customer's specific concerns and providing relevant information.

Personalizing Responses

Personalization enhances the customer experience and builds a stronger connection between your brand and your audience. When responding to inquiries, use the customer's name and refer to their specific issue or question to make the interaction feel more individualized.

Tailor your responses based on the context of the inquiry. For example, if a customer asks about a product they purchased, provide information related to that product, such as usage tips, care instructions, or troubleshooting advice. Avoid generic replies that do not address the customer's unique situation, as these can come across as impersonal and unhelpful.

If a customer has had a previous interaction with your brand, reference it in your response. This shows that you are attentive to their history and adds a personal touch to the conversation. For instance, if a customer previously expressed interest in a specific product, you could mention this when addressing their current inquiry.

Handling Complaints and Negative Feedback

Effectively managing complaints and negative feedback is vital for maintaining customer trust and improving your brand's reputation. Approach these interactions with empathy, understanding, and a problem-solving mindset.

When handling complaints, acknowledge the customer's issue and express genuine concern. Use empathetic language to validate their feelings and reassure them that their concerns are taken seriously. For example, you might say, "I'm sorry to hear about your experience, and I understand how frustrating this must be for you."

Offer a solution or next steps to resolve the issue. Depending on the nature of the complaint, this might involve issuing a refund, providing a replacement, or offering additional support. Ensure that the resolution is fair and aligns with your company's policies. Communicate what actions will be taken and follow up to confirm that the customer is satisfied with the resolution.

Additionally, use negative feedback as an opportunity for improvement. Analyze the feedback to identify recurring issues or areas where your products or services may need enhancement. Implementing changes based on customer input can help prevent future complaints and demonstrate your commitment to continuous improvement.

Encouraging and Collecting Positive Feedback

Encouraging and collecting positive feedback is equally important as managing complaints. Positive feedback not only reinforces customer satisfaction but also provides valuable testimonials that can enhance your brand's credibility.

Encourage customers to share their positive experiences by directly asking for feedback after a purchase or interaction. For example, you might send a follow-up message thanking them for their purchase and inviting them to share their thoughts. You could also incentivize feedback by offering a small discount or entry into a giveaway for those who provide reviews or testimonials.

Make it easy for customers to leave feedback by providing clear instructions and multiple options. You can request feedback through WhatsApp itself, or direct customers to online review platforms or survey forms. Ensure that the feedback process is simple and quick, reducing any potential friction for the customer.

Leveraging Feedback for Improvement

Collecting feedback is just the beginning; using it effectively is key to making meaningful improvements. Regularly review the feedback you receive to identify trends, strengths, and areas for improvement. This analysis can provide insights into customer preferences, satisfaction levels, and potential pain points.

Share feedback with relevant teams within your organization to drive improvements. For instance, if customers frequently mention issues with product quality or service delivery, address these concerns with your product development or operations teams. Using feedback to inform decision-making can lead to enhanced products, better customer experiences, and increased overall satisfaction.

Communicate any changes or improvements made as a result of customer feedback. Letting customers know that their input has led to tangible changes demonstrates that you value their opinions and are committed to meeting their needs.

Maintaining a Professional and Friendly Tone

Regardless of the nature of the inquiry or feedback, maintaining a professional and friendly tone is essential for positive customer interactions. Use courteous language, be respectful, and show appreciation for the customer's engagement.

Incorporate a warm and personable touch in your responses to create a positive experience. Avoid overly formal or robotic language, and instead, aim for a conversational tone that reflects your brand's personality. For instance, instead of saying, "Your complaint has been received," you might say, "Thank you for bringing this to our attention. We're here to help and will work to resolve this issue for you."

Handling customer inquiries and feedback effectively on WhatsApp involves prompt responses, personalization, and a proactive approach to complaints and positive feedback. By creating a system for managing inquiries, personalizing interactions, addressing complaints with empathy, and leveraging feedback for improvement, you can enhance customer satisfaction and strengthen your brand's reputation. Maintaining a professional and friendly tone throughout your communications will further ensure that every interaction contributes positively to your overall customer experience. In the next section, we will delve into advanced techniques for analyzing and optimizing your WhatsApp marketing performance.

Chapter 5: Creating Engaging Content for WhatsApp

Creating engaging content is essential for maximizing the impact of your WhatsApp marketing efforts. Unlike traditional marketing channels, WhatsApp offers a more personal and interactive experience, making it crucial to craft content that resonates with your audience and encourages active engagement. This chapter explores strategies for developing compelling content that captures attention, drives interaction, and builds lasting connections with your customers.

1. Understanding WhatsApp's Content Capabilities

WhatsApp's content capabilities extend beyond simple text messages, offering a range of formats to enhance your communication strategy. Understanding these capabilities allows you to utilize the platform's full potential and create diverse and engaging content.

- **Text Messages**: The core of WhatsApp communication is text messaging. Crafting clear, concise, and compelling text messages is crucial. Use conversational language that aligns with your brand's voice to make messages more relatable. Ensure that your texts are actionable, providing clear calls to action, whether it's directing users to a website, encouraging them to reply, or inviting them to participate in a promotion.
- **Images and Videos**: Visual content, including images and videos, can significantly boost engagement. Use high-quality images that are relevant to your message and visually appealing. Videos can be used for product demonstrations, behind-the-scenes looks, or customer testimonials. Short, engaging videos are often more

effective than lengthy ones, as they cater to the quick-consumption nature of mobile content.

- **Voice Messages**: Voice messages offer a personal touch and can be particularly effective for conveying emotion or providing detailed explanations. Use voice messages to deliver personalized greetings, provide customer support, or share exclusive content. Keep them brief and focused to maintain listener interest.

- **Documents and Files**: WhatsApp allows you to share documents and files, which can be useful for sending brochures, reports, or detailed product information. Ensure that the files are well-organized and easily accessible, and provide context for why the recipient might find them valuable.

- **Interactive Content**: Utilize interactive elements such as polls and surveys to engage your audience. These features encourage participation and provide valuable insights into customer preferences and opinions. Interactive content can be used to gather feedback, conduct market research, or simply engage users in a fun and engaging way.

2. Crafting Compelling Messages

To capture attention and encourage engagement, your WhatsApp messages must be compelling and tailored to your audience's interests and needs.

- **Start with a Strong Opening**: The first few lines of your message are crucial for grabbing attention. Begin with a hook that piques curiosity or addresses a pain point. For example, if you're promoting a sale, start with something like, "Exclusive offer just for you – save 20% on your favorite items today!"

- **Be Clear and Concise**: WhatsApp users often skim through messages, so keep your content brief and to the point. Avoid long paragraphs and use bullet points or line breaks to make the message easier to read. Focus on delivering the key information quickly and clearly.
- **Include a Clear Call to Action**: Every message should have a purpose and guide the recipient on what to do next. Whether it's visiting a website, replying to a message, or taking advantage of an offer, ensure your call to action is clear and compelling. For example, "Click here to shop now and enjoy 10% off your purchase."
- **Personalize Your Messages**: Personalization can significantly enhance engagement. Use the recipient's name, refer to their previous interactions, and tailor the content to their interests or preferences. This approach makes the message feel more relevant and valued.
- **Use Emojis and Formatting Wisely**: Emojis can add a friendly and engaging touch to your messages. Use them to convey emotions or highlight important points, but avoid overusing them, as it can detract from the message's professionalism. Similarly, use formatting options like bold or italics to emphasize key information, but ensure it enhances readability without overwhelming the recipient.

3. Leveraging Content for Different Stages of the Customer Journey

Tailoring your content to different stages of the customer journey ensures that your messages are relevant and timely, enhancing their effectiveness.

- **Awareness Stage**: At this stage, your content should focus on introducing your brand and providing value. Share informative and engaging content that addresses common problems or interests of your target audience. This could include educational articles, introductory videos, or engaging infographics.
- **Consideration Stage**: In the consideration stage, your content should help prospects evaluate your products or services. Provide detailed information, customer testimonials, and case studies to build trust and demonstrate the benefits of what you offer. Highlight key features, provide comparisons, and offer free trials or demos if applicable.
- **Decision Stage**: Content at this stage should focus on encouraging the final decision to purchase or take action. Use persuasive messages, exclusive offers, and urgent calls to action to drive conversions. Personalized offers or discounts can be particularly effective in motivating customers to make a purchase.
- **Post-Purchase Stage**: After a purchase, continue engaging with your customers to build loyalty and encourage repeat business. Send thank-you messages, request feedback, and offer support. Share tips on how to use the product effectively or provide exclusive offers for future purchases.

4. Testing and Optimizing Content

Continuous testing and optimization are key to improving the effectiveness of your WhatsApp content. Regularly review the performance of your messages and make data-driven adjustments to enhance engagement and results.

- **Monitor Performance Metrics**: Track metrics such as open rates, click-through rates, and response rates to evaluate the effectiveness of your content. Use this data to identify which types of content resonate most with your audience and which areas need improvement.

- **Conduct A/B Testing**: A/B testing involves creating multiple versions of a message to see which performs better. Test different elements, such as message tone, call-to-action phrasing, or visual content, to determine what drives the best results. Use the insights gained from testing to refine your content strategy.

- **Gather Customer Feedback**: Actively seek feedback from your audience on the content you share. Use surveys or direct interactions to understand what they find valuable and engaging. Incorporate their feedback into your content strategy to better meet their needs and preferences.

- **Adjust Based on Insights**: Use the data and feedback collected to make informed adjustments to your content. Continuously refine your messaging, visuals, and calls to action to align with audience preferences and improve overall engagement.

Creating engaging content for WhatsApp involves understanding the platform's capabilities, crafting compelling messages, tailoring content to different stages of the customer journey, and continuously testing and optimizing. By leveraging WhatsApp's diverse content formats, personalizing interactions, and aligning your content with customer needs, you can effectively capture attention, drive engagement, and build stronger connections with your audience. In the next chapter, we will explore advanced techniques for measuring and analyzing the success of your WhatsApp marketing campaigns.

5.1 Types of Content: Text, Images, Videos, and More

WhatsApp supports various types of content, each offering unique opportunities to engage with your audience effectively. Understanding the strengths and best practices for each type can help you create a diverse and impactful content strategy. This section explores the different content formats available on WhatsApp and guides how to use them to maximize engagement and communication.

Text Messages

Text messages form the foundation of WhatsApp communication and remain a primary method for delivering content. Crafting effective text messages involves focusing on clarity, conciseness, and engagement.

- **Crafting Engaging Texts**: Start with a compelling opening to grab the recipient's attention. Keep your messages brief and focused, avoiding lengthy paragraphs. Use conversational language that aligns with your brand's tone and makes the message feel personal and relatable. Ensure each message has a clear call-to-action, guiding recipients on the next steps.
- **Personalization**: Personalizing text messages enhances their relevance and impact. Use the recipient's name and reference their previous interactions or preferences. Tailor your messages to address specific needs or interests, which can increase engagement and response rates.
- **Formatting**: WhatsApp allows basic text formatting such as bold, italics, and strikethrough. Use these formatting options to highlight

important points or emphasize key information. However, avoid excessive formatting, which can make the text harder to read.

Images

Images are a powerful way to capture attention and convey visual information quickly. They can be used to enhance text messages, showcase products, or create visually appealing content.

- **High-Quality Visuals**: Use high-resolution images that are clear and visually appealing. Images should be relevant to the message and align with your brand's aesthetic. For product promotions, ensure that the images highlight key features and benefits.
- **Context and Relevance**: Provide context for the images you share. Accompany images with descriptive text or captions that explain their relevance and encourage engagement. For example, if sharing a promotional image, include details about the offer and a call to action.
- **Variety**: Incorporate a mix of images to keep your content fresh and engaging. This could include product photos, infographics, behind-the-scenes shots, or user-generated content. Variety helps maintain interest and caters to different preferences.

Videos

Videos are an effective medium for delivering dynamic and engaging content. They can be used to demonstrate products, share stories, or provide informative content in a more engaging format than text alone.

- **Video Length and Quality**: Keep videos short and focused, ideally under one minute. Shorter videos are more likely to be watched in full and are better suited for mobile consumption. Ensure that videos are high-quality with good lighting and clear audio.
- **Content Types**: Use videos for a range of purposes, such as product demonstrations, customer testimonials, tutorials, or event highlights. Tailor the video content to the interests and needs of your audience. For example, a how-to video can provide value by demonstrating how to use a product effectively.
- **Call-to-Action**: Include a clear call-to-action in your videos. Whether it's directing viewers to a website, encouraging them to reply to the message, or prompting them to take advantage of an offer, ensure that the next steps are clear and compelling.

Voice Messages

Voice messages offer a personal touch and can be an effective way to convey information or emotions that might be lost in text. They are particularly useful for direct communication and providing detailed explanations.

- **Personalization and Tone**: Use voice messages to create a more personal connection with your audience. Speak clearly and warmly, and use a friendly tone that aligns with your brand's voice. Personalize the message by addressing the recipient by name and referring to their specific query or interaction.
- **Brevity**: Keep voice messages brief and to the point. Aim for messages that are no longer than 30 seconds to maintain the recipient's attention and ensure that the content is easily digestible.

- **Use Cases**: Voice messages can be used for a variety of purposes, including delivering personalized greetings, providing quick updates, or addressing customer support queries. They are also useful for conveying complex information that may be challenging to explain in text.

Documents and Files

WhatsApp allows you to share various types of documents and files, which can be useful for providing detailed information or resources.

- **Types of Documents**: Share files such as brochures, product catalogs, reports, or user manuals to provide additional information or resources. Ensure that documents are well-organized and relevant to the recipient's interests or needs.
- **File Size and Format**: Keep file sizes manageable to ensure quick and easy access for recipients. Use common file formats such as PDFs for documents, which are widely accessible and easy to view on mobile devices.
- **Context and Instructions**: Provide context for the documents you share by including a brief explanation of their contents and how they can be used. This helps recipients understand the value of the documents and encourages them to review and engage with the content.

Interactive Content

Interactive content, such as polls and surveys, can drive engagement and provide valuable insights into your audience's preferences and opinions.

- **Polls**: Use polls to gather quick feedback or gauge interest in specific topics. Polls can be a fun and engaging way to involve your audience and make them feel more connected to your brand.
- **Surveys**: Conduct surveys to gather more detailed feedback or conduct market research. Surveys can help you understand customer satisfaction, identify areas for improvement, and gather insights into customer needs and preferences.
- **Engagement**: Encourage participation by making interactive content easy to access and respond to. Keep questions clear and concise, and ensure that the process is user-friendly to maximize participation.

Understanding and utilizing the different types of content available on WhatsApp—text messages, images, videos, voice messages, documents, and interactive content—allows you to create a diverse and engaging content strategy. Each type of content has its strengths and can be used to achieve different objectives, from capturing attention to driving action. By leveraging these content formats effectively and tailoring them to your audience's preferences, you can enhance your WhatsApp marketing efforts and build stronger connections with your customers. In the next section, we will explore strategies for creating a content calendar and managing content delivery to ensure consistency and effectiveness.

5.2 Writing Effective WhatsApp Messages

Writing effective WhatsApp messages is crucial for capturing attention, conveying your message clearly, and encouraging engagement. The nature of WhatsApp as a personal and direct communication platform means that your messages should be crafted with care to ensure they are impactful and well-received. This section provides guidelines and best practices for writing messages that resonate with your audience and achieve your marketing objectives.

Crafting Attention-Grabbing Openings

The opening lines of your WhatsApp messages are critical for grabbing the recipient's attention. Given that users often skim through messages, a strong opening helps ensure your message stands out.

- **Start with a Hook**: Begin with a compelling statement or question that piques curiosity or addresses a pain point. For instance, instead of starting with "We have a new sale," try "Don't miss out on our exclusive 30% discount just for you!" This approach immediately highlights the value of the message.
- **Personalize the Greeting**: Address the recipient by name if possible. Personalized greetings make the message feel more tailored and relevant. For example, "Hi Sarah, we've got something special for you!" is more engaging than a generic "Hello."

Maintaining Clarity and Brevity

WhatsApp messages should be clear and concise to ensure that your key points are easily understood and quickly absorbed.

- **Be Direct**: Get to the point quickly. Avoid lengthy introductions or unnecessary details that might dilute the main message. Focus on delivering your core message in a straightforward manner.
- **Use Simple Language**: Choose simple and straightforward language that is easy to understand. Avoid jargon or complex terms that could confuse the recipient. For example, instead of "avail yourself of our latest promotions," use "check out our latest deals."
- **Break Up Text**: Use short paragraphs or bullet points to break up text and make it more digestible. Long blocks of text can be overwhelming and may lead to reduced engagement. Formatting your message with line breaks or bullet points helps improve readability.

Incorporating Clear Calls to Action

A clear and compelling call to action (CTA) directs the recipient on what to do next and encourages them to take the desired action.

- **Make CTAs Stand Out**: Use actionable language that communicates what you want the recipient to do. Phrases like "Shop Now," "Reply to this message," or "Click the link to learn more" are effective CTAs. Ensure that the CTA is prominent and easy to follow.

- **Create Urgency**: Encourage prompt action by incorporating a sense of urgency in your CTA. For instance, "Hurry, offer ends tonight!" or "Limited spots available—reserve yours now!" This approach can drive immediate responses and engagement.
- **Provide Clear Instructions**: If your CTA involves a multi-step process, provide clear instructions to guide the recipient. For example, if asking them to visit a website, include a direct link and brief instructions on what they should do once they arrive at the site.

Personalizing and Targeting Messages

Personalization helps make your messages more relevant and engaging by tailoring them to the recipient's interests and previous interactions.

- **Use Recipient Data**: Leverage available data such as the recipient's name, purchase history, or preferences to personalize messages. For example, "Hi John, based on your recent purchase, we thought you'd love our new product line."
- **Segment Your Audience**: Segment your audience based on criteria like demographics, behavior, or interests. Tailor your messages to each segment to ensure they are relevant and appealing. For instance, send different offers to new customers compared to loyal, repeat buyers.
- **Respond to Previous Interactions**: Reference past interactions to create a more personalized experience. For example, "Thanks for your feedback on our last product. We're excited to share our latest update with you!"

Using Emojis and Formatting Effectively

Emojis and formatting can enhance your messages by adding visual interest and emphasizing key points. However, they should be used thoughtfully to maintain professionalism.

- **Enhance with Emojis**: Use emojis to add a friendly tone and draw attention to important parts of your message. For instance, a shopping bag emoji can emphasize a special offer, while a thumbs-up emoji can express appreciation. Avoid overusing emojis, which can clutter the message and reduce its effectiveness.
- **Employ Formatting**: Use WhatsApp's formatting options—bold, italics, and strikethrough—to highlight important information or create emphasis. For example, use bold text to draw attention to a special offer or italics for emphasis. Ensure that formatting enhances readability and doesn't distract from the message.

Testing and Iterating

Regularly testing and iterating on your WhatsApp messages can help you refine your approach and improve effectiveness.

- **A/B Testing**: Experiment with different message formats, openings, CTAs, or tones to see what resonates best with your audience. A/B testing allows you to compare different versions and determine which one drives better engagement and responses.
- **Monitor Performance**: Track metrics such as open rates, response rates, and click-through rates to evaluate the success of your

messages. Use this data to identify trends, understand audience preferences, and make data-driven adjustments to your messaging strategy.

- **Gather Feedback**: Collect feedback from recipients to gain insights into their preferences and perceptions. Use this feedback to refine your messaging approach and better meet your audience's needs.

Writing effective WhatsApp messages involves crafting attention-grabbing openings, maintaining clarity and brevity, incorporating clear calls to action, personalizing content, and using emojis and formatting thoughtfully. By following these best practices, you can create messages that resonate with your audience, drive engagement, and achieve your marketing goals. Continuous testing and iteration will further enhance your messaging strategy and ensure that your content remains relevant and impactful. In the next chapter, we will explore advanced strategies for leveraging WhatsApp's features to maximize your marketing efforts.

5.3 Visual Storytelling: Designing Eye-Catching Media

Visual storytelling is a powerful approach to engaging your audience on WhatsApp. It leverages images, videos, and other visual elements to convey messages compellingly and memorably. Effective visual storytelling can captivate attention, enhance brand perception, and drive interaction. This section delves into the key principles and best practices for designing eye-catching media that resonates with your audience.

Understanding Visual Storytelling

Visual storytelling involves using visual elements to communicate a narrative or message. It combines images, videos, and graphics to create a cohesive story that captures the audience's attention and elicits an emotional response.

- **The Power of Visuals**: Humans process visuals faster than text, making them a powerful tool for conveying information quickly and effectively. Visual storytelling helps simplify complex messages, evoke emotions, and create a lasting impact. For example, a well-designed infographic can present data in a more engaging way than a text-heavy report.
- **Consistency and Branding**: Consistent use of visual elements helps reinforce your brand identity and makes your content recognizable. Use your brand's colors, fonts, and style consistently across all visual media to create a cohesive and professional look.

Designing Eye-Catching Images

Images are a key component of visual storytelling and can be used to enhance your messages, highlight products, or convey emotions.

- **High-Quality Imagery**: Use high-resolution images that are clear and visually appealing. Poor-quality images can detract from your message and negatively impact your brand's perception. Invest in professional photography or high-quality stock images that align with your brand's aesthetic.

- **Visual Hierarchy**: Organize visual elements to guide the viewer's eye and emphasize key information. Use contrasting colors, sizes, and placements to create a visual hierarchy that directs attention to the most important aspects of the image.
- **Relevance and Context**: Ensure that images are relevant to your message and context. For instance, if promoting a new product, use images that showcase the product in use or highlight its key features. Provide context through captions or accompanying text to enhance the viewer's understanding.

Creating Engaging Videos

Videos offer dynamic and engaging ways to tell a story and communicate your message. They can be used for product demonstrations, customer testimonials, or brand storytelling.

- **Video Quality and Length**: Ensure that your videos are high-quality, with clear visuals and audio. Keep videos short and focused, ideally under one minute, to maintain viewer interest. Short videos are better suited for mobile consumption and quick engagement.
- **Storytelling Techniques**: Use storytelling techniques to create compelling videos. Develop a narrative that captures attention and maintains engagement throughout the video. Incorporate elements such as a clear beginning, middle, and end to structure the video effectively.
- **Calls to Action**: Include clear calls to action in your videos to guide viewers on what to do next. Whether it's visiting a website, signing up for a promotion, or sharing a video, ensure that the CTA is prominent and easy to follow.

Leveraging Graphics and Infographics

Graphics and infographics can help convey complex information in a visually appealing and easily digestible format.

- **Infographic Design**: Create infographics that present data or information in a visually engaging way. Use charts, icons, and illustrations to break down complex data and make it more accessible. Ensure that infographics are well-organized and easy to read.
- **Graphic Elements**: Use graphic elements such as icons, overlays, and frames to enhance your visual content. These elements can help highlight key points, add visual interest, and reinforce your brand's style.
- **Consistency and Simplicity**: Maintain consistency in your graphic design to align with your brand's visual identity. Avoid cluttering graphics with excessive information or decorative elements. Keep designs simple and focused on the core message.

Utilizing WhatsApp Features for Visual Content

WhatsApp offers several features that can enhance the presentation and effectiveness of your visual content.

- **Status Updates**: Use WhatsApp Status updates to share short-lived visual content such as promotions, events, or behind-the-scenes glimpses. Status updates can be a great way to reach your audience with timely and engaging visuals.

- **Media Sharing**: Share images, videos, and documents directly in chat to provide additional context or information. Use media sharing to supplement text messages and enhance the overall messaging experience.
- **Stickers and GIFs**: Incorporate stickers and GIFs to add a fun and interactive element to your messages. These features can help convey emotions or reactions and make your content more engaging.

Measuring and Optimizing Visual Content

Regularly assess the performance of your visual content to ensure it meets your objectives and resonates with your audience.

- **Performance Metrics**: Track metrics such as engagement rates, views, and shares to evaluate the effectiveness of your visual content. Use these metrics to understand what types of visuals perform best and where improvements can be made.
- **Feedback and Iteration**: Gather feedback from your audience to gain insights into their preferences and perceptions. Use this feedback to refine your visual content strategy and make data-driven adjustments to enhance its impact.

Effective visual storytelling involves designing eye-catching media that captures attention, conveys messages clearly, and engages your audience. By leveraging high-quality images, engaging videos, informative graphics, and WhatsApp's features, you can create compelling visual content that enhances your marketing efforts. Consistency in design, relevance to your message, and continuous optimization will help you create impactful visual stories that resonate with your audience and drive engagement. In the next chapter, we will explore strategies for analyzing and measuring the success of your WhatsApp marketing campaigns.

5.4 Using Emojis and Stickers to Enhance Communication

Emojis and stickers have become integral elements of digital communication, adding personality, emotion, and context to messages. On WhatsApp, these visual tools can significantly enhance the effectiveness of your marketing efforts by making messages more engaging, relatable, and expressive. This section explores how to effectively use emojis and stickers in your WhatsApp marketing to strengthen your connection with your audience.

The Role of Emojis in Communication

Emojis serve as visual cues that can express emotions, tone, and context that might otherwise be lost in text-only messages. They are small but powerful tools for humanizing your brand and creating a more engaging and relatable communication style.

- **Enhancing Tone and Emotion**: Emojis can transform the tone of your message, making it more friendly, playful, or empathetic. For instance, adding a smiley face at the end of a sentence can make your message feel warm and approachable. Emojis help convey emotions that might be ambiguous in plain text, ensuring that your message is received in the intended tone.

- **Breaking the Ice**: Emojis can make your messages feel less formal and more conversational, which is particularly useful when initiating contact or making cold outreach. A well-placed emoji can break the ice and make your audience feel more comfortable engaging with your content.
- **Improving Readability**: Emojis can also help break up text and make your messages easier to read. They can act as visual separators, guiding the reader's eye to key points or highlighting important information. For example, using a checkmark next to a key benefit can draw attention to it.

Best Practices for Using Emojis

While emojis can enhance communication, it's important to use them thoughtfully to avoid overuse or miscommunication.

- **Contextual Relevance**: Ensure that the emojis you use are relevant to the message and context. An emoji should complement the text, not distract from it. For instance, using a celebratory emoji like is appropriate when announcing a sale or milestone, but might be out of place in a more serious context.
- **Consistency with Brand Voice**: Align your emoji usage with your brand's tone and personality. If your brand has a playful, casual tone, a wider range of emojis might be appropriate. For a more formal brand, emoji usage might be limited to more neutral or minimal expressions, like a simple thumbs-up.
- **Avoid Overuse**: While emojis can add flair to your messages, overusing them can clutter your communication and make it seem unprofessional. Aim for a balanced approach—use emojis to

enhance key points, but ensure the main message remains clear and focused.

- **Cultural Sensitivity**: Be mindful of cultural differences in emoji interpretation. Some emojis might have different meanings in different cultures, so it's important to consider your audience's background to avoid unintended connotations.

The Impact of Stickers on WhatsApp Marketing

Stickers are larger, more detailed visual elements than emojis and can convey more complex messages or emotions. WhatsApp stickers offer a creative way to engage your audience, often in a fun and memorable way.

- **Brand-Specific Stickers**: WhatsApp allows businesses to create and share their own branded sticker packs. This is a unique opportunity to enhance brand identity and provide your audience with a new way to interact with your brand. For instance, if you run a food delivery service, you could create stickers featuring your mascot or popular dishes.
- **Storytelling and Engagement**: Stickers can be used to tell a story or convey a message in a visually engaging way. For example, a series of stickers could depict the journey of a product from creation to delivery, enhancing the customer's experience and connection with your brand.
- **Adding Personality**: Stickers allow you to inject personality into your communication, making interactions more memorable. They can be particularly effective in customer service interactions, where a friendly sticker can help turn a routine message into a delightful experience.

Best Practices for Using Stickers

To maximize the impact of stickers in your WhatsApp marketing, consider the following guidelines:

- **Relevance and Timing**: Like emojis, stickers should be used when they are relevant and add value to the message. Consider the timing of your sticker use—whether it's to celebrate a customer milestone, express gratitude, or inject humor into a conversation, the sticker should enhance the interaction.
- **Create a Branded Sticker Pack**: If appropriate for your brand, consider developing a custom sticker pack that your audience can use. This not only boosts brand recognition but also fosters a sense of community as customers share your stickers with others. Ensure the designs are high-quality and reflect your brand's values and aesthetic.
- **Encourage User-Generated Stickers**: Engage your audience by encouraging them to create and share their stickers related to your brand or products. This can be part of a contest or campaign, increasing brand engagement and visibility.
- **Avoid Overdoing It**: Similar to emojis, overusing stickers can dilute their impact. Use them sparingly to maintain their novelty and effectiveness. Stickers should be seen as a special addition to your messages, not a replacement for clear communication.

Combining Emojis and Stickers for Maximum Impact

Using emojis and stickers together can create a dynamic and engaging communication style that resonates with your audience. For instance, an emoji can set the tone for a message, while a sticker can deliver the punchline or emphasize a key point.

- **Creating a Visual Flow**: Combine emojis and stickers to create a visual flow in your messages. Start with an emoji to introduce a concept or emotion, and follow up with a sticker to reinforce or conclude the message. This layered approach can make your communication more memorable.
- **Segmented Messaging**: Use emojis to segment different parts of your message, then cap off with a relevant sticker that ties the entire message together. For example, you might use a series of emojis to list out the benefits of a new product and conclude with a celebratory sticker to emphasize excitement.
- **Feedback and Interaction**: Encourage your audience to respond with their emojis and stickers, creating an interactive and engaging conversation. This can be particularly effective in group chats or during promotional campaigns where customer participation is key.

Emojis and stickers are powerful tools for enhancing communication on WhatsApp. When used effectively, they can add emotion, personality, and visual interest to your messages, making them more engaging and impactful. By understanding the best practices for using these visual elements, you can create a more dynamic and relatable communication style that resonates with your audience and strengthens your brand's presence on WhatsApp. In the next chapter, we will explore how to analyze and measure the effectiveness of your WhatsApp marketing efforts to optimize future campaigns.

Chapter 6: WhatsApp Campaigns: Planning and Execution

WhatsApp has emerged as a powerful platform for running targeted marketing campaigns, thanks to its extensive reach, high engagement rates, and personal nature. However, the success of a WhatsApp campaign hinges on careful planning, strategic execution, and continuous optimization. This chapter will guide you through the essential steps for planning and executing effective WhatsApp marketing campaigns that drive results and resonate with your audience.

1. Understanding the Essentials of a WhatsApp Campaign

A WhatsApp campaign is a coordinated marketing effort aimed at achieving specific business objectives using the features and tools offered by WhatsApp. Whether you're launching a new product, promoting a sale, or nurturing customer relationships, a WhatsApp campaign can be a highly effective way to connect with your audience.

Key elements of a successful WhatsApp campaign include setting clear goals, defining your target audience, crafting compelling messages, and leveraging the platform's unique features such as groups, broadcasts, and WhatsApp Status.

- **Campaign Goals**: Before you start planning your campaign, define your objectives. Are you aiming to increase sales, drive website traffic, build brand awareness, or improve customer retention? Clear goals will guide your campaign strategy and help you measure success.

- **Audience Segmentation**: Understanding your target audience is crucial for tailoring your campaign messages. Segment your audience based on demographics, behavior, purchase history, or engagement level. This allows you to create personalized messages that resonate with different segments.

- **Message Crafting**: Your campaign's success largely depends on the quality and relevance of your messages. Craft concise, engaging, and actionable messages that align with your campaign objectives. Use a mix of text, images, videos, and links to create a rich messaging experience.

- **Feature Utilization**: Leverage WhatsApp's features to enhance your campaign. Use broadcast lists to send messages to large groups without losing the personal touch, create engaging content for WhatsApp Status, and consider using WhatsApp Business API for more advanced campaign capabilities.

2. Developing a Comprehensive Campaign Plan

A well-structured campaign plan serves as the blueprint for your WhatsApp marketing efforts. It should outline your campaign objectives, target audience, messaging strategy, timeline, and metrics for success.

- **Campaign Timeline**: Establish a clear timeline for your campaign, including the launch date, key milestones, and the end date. This helps ensure that your campaign stays on track and allows you to monitor progress effectively. Consider the timing of your messages to maximize engagement—sending messages during peak hours when your audience is most active can lead to higher response rates.

- **Content Calendar**: Create a content calendar that details what content will be sent, when, and to whom. This ensures consistency and helps you manage the flow of communication. Your content calendar should align with your broader marketing strategy and account for any important dates, holidays, or events that may impact your campaign.
- **Message Frequency**: Determine the frequency of your messages to avoid overwhelming your audience. Striking a balance between staying top-of-mind and avoiding message fatigue is crucial. Consider staggering your messages or using drip campaigns to maintain engagement over time.
- **Budgeting and Resources**: Allocate a budget for your WhatsApp campaign if necessary, especially if you're using the WhatsApp Business API, which may involve costs for sending messages or integrating with other platforms. Ensure that you have the necessary resources, including staff and tools, to execute the campaign effectively.

3. Crafting and Delivering Impactful Campaign Messages

The effectiveness of your WhatsApp campaign hinges on the quality and delivery of your messages. Crafting impactful messages that resonate with your audience is key to achieving your campaign objectives.

- **Personalization**: Personalize your messages to make your audience feel valued. Use their names, reference past interactions, or tailor the message content based on their preferences. Personalization increases the likelihood of engagement and conversion.

- **Value Proposition**: Communicate the value of your offer. Whether it's a discount, a limited-time offer, or valuable content, ensure that the recipient understands what's in it for them. Highlight the benefits and use persuasive language to encourage action.

- **Call to Action (CTA)**: Every campaign message should include a clear and compelling call to action. Whether you want recipients to make a purchase, visit your website, or reply to your message, the CTA should be easy to understand and act upon.

- **Multimedia Elements**: Incorporate images, videos, and links to enhance your messages. Visual content can make your messages more engaging and memorable. For example, a short video demonstrating a product can be more effective than a text description alone.

- **Testing and Optimization**: Test different versions of your messages to see what resonates best with your audience. A/B testing can help you refine your messaging strategy by comparing different text, images, or CTAs. Use the insights gained to optimize future messages.

4. Monitoring and Analyzing Campaign Performance

Monitoring and analyzing the performance of your WhatsApp campaign is essential for understanding its effectiveness and making data-driven decisions for future campaigns.

- **Key Metrics**: Track key metrics such as open rates, response rates, click-through rates, and conversion rates. These metrics provide insights into how well your campaign is performing and where improvements can be made. For example, a high open rate but low click-through rate may indicate that your message is engaging but the CTA needs refinement.

- **Audience Feedback**: Pay attention to the feedback you receive from your audience. This can include direct responses to your messages, as well as broader trends in engagement or sentiment. Audience feedback can provide valuable insights into what's working and what's not, allowing you to adjust your campaign strategy accordingly.

- **Campaign Adjustments**: Based on your analysis, make any necessary adjustments to your campaign. This could involve tweaking your messaging, adjusting your target audience, or changing the timing of your messages. Continuous optimization is key to maximizing the success of your campaign.

- **Reporting and Insights**: Compile your findings into a comprehensive campaign report. This should include an overview of key metrics, insights gained, and recommendations for future campaigns. Use this report to inform your broader marketing strategy and share learnings with your team.

5. Case Studies and Examples of Successful WhatsApp Campaigns

Learning from successful WhatsApp campaigns can provide valuable insights and inspiration for your own efforts. This section will explore several case studies of brands that have effectively utilized WhatsApp for marketing campaigns, highlighting key strategies and takeaways.

- **Brand X**: Launching a New Product: Explore how Brand X used WhatsApp to successfully launch a new product, from building anticipation with teasers to driving sales with exclusive offers. Key takeaways include the importance of timing, exclusivity, and leveraging multimedia content.

- **Brand Y**: Customer Retention Campaign: Learn how Brand Y used WhatsApp to re-engage lapsed customers and improve retention rates. The case study will cover strategies such as personalized messaging, targeted offers, and the use of WhatsApp Status to keep customers informed and engaged.
- **Brand Z**: Event Promotion: Discover how Brand Z utilized WhatsApp to promote an event, driving ticket sales and attendee engagement. The case study will highlight the role of WhatsApp groups, real-time updates, and interactive content in creating a successful event campaign.

Planning and executing a successful WhatsApp campaign requires a strategic approach, from setting clear goals and crafting compelling messages to leveraging the platform's features and continuously optimizing performance. By following the guidelines and best practices outlined in this chapter, you can create WhatsApp campaigns that effectively engage your audience, drive results, and contribute to your overall marketing success. In the next chapter, we will explore advanced strategies for integrating WhatsApp with other marketing channels to create a cohesive and omnichannel marketing approach.

6.1 Types of Campaigns: Promotions, Announcements, Surveys

WhatsApp offers a versatile platform for running a variety of marketing campaigns, each tailored to achieve specific objectives. Understanding the different types of campaigns you can run on WhatsApp will help you leverage the platform's strengths and create targeted strategies that resonate with your audience. In this section, we will explore three common types of WhatsApp campaigns: Promotions, Announcements, and Surveys.

Promotional Campaigns

Promotional campaigns are designed to drive sales, boost brand awareness, or introduce new products or services. WhatsApp's direct and personal communication style makes it an ideal platform for running promotions that feel exclusive and targeted.

- **Exclusive Offers and Discounts**: One of the most effective ways to engage your audience on WhatsApp is by offering exclusive deals or discounts that are only available to your WhatsApp contacts. This creates a sense of exclusivity and urgency, encouraging recipients to take action quickly. For example, you could send a limited-time discount code to your WhatsApp list, driving immediate sales and fostering loyalty among your audience.
- **Product Launches**: WhatsApp is an excellent platform for launching new products or services. You can build anticipation by sending sneak peeks, teaser videos, or countdown messages leading up to the launch. On the day of the launch, you can send a personalized message with a direct link to purchase or learn more about the product. This approach not only drives traffic but also creates a buzz around your new offerings.
- **Flash Sales and Time-Sensitive Offers**: The immediacy of WhatsApp makes it perfect for promoting flash sales or time-sensitive offers. By sending out a message that highlights a limited-time sale, you can capitalize on the urgency and prompt

quick responses from your audience. Use engaging visuals and clear calls to action (CTAs) to ensure your message stands out and drives conversions.

- **Upselling and Cross-Selling**: Promotional campaigns on WhatsApp can also be used to upsell or cross-sell products to your existing customers. By analyzing purchase history and preferences, you can send targeted messages that suggest complementary products or upgrades, increasing your average order value and deepening customer relationships.

Announcement Campaigns

Announcement campaigns are focused on delivering important news or updates to your audience. These campaigns help keep your audience informed and engaged, ensuring they are always up-to-date with your brand's latest developments.

- **Company News and Updates**: Keeping your audience informed about major changes or updates within your company is crucial for maintaining transparency and trust. Whether it's a new partnership, a change in business hours, or an update on company policies, WhatsApp allows you to deliver these messages directly to your audience in a timely and personalized manner.
- **Event Invitations and Reminders**: WhatsApp is an effective tool for sending invitations to events such as webinars, product launches, or in-store promotions. You can use WhatsApp to send event details, RSVP links, and reminders as the event date approaches. This not only boosts attendance but also ensures that your audience feels personally invited and valued.

- **New Content Announcements**: If your brand regularly produces content such as blog posts, videos, or newsletters, WhatsApp is an excellent platform for sharing new releases with your audience. You can send summaries or highlights of the content, along with a direct link to access it. This drives traffic to your content and keeps your audience engaged with your brand's thought leadership.
- **Product or Service Updates**: Use WhatsApp to announce updates or improvements to your products or services. Whether it's a new feature, a software update, or an expansion of your service offerings, keeping your customers informed ensures they continue to see the value in your brand. Clear communication through WhatsApp can help mitigate any potential confusion and enhance customer satisfaction.

Survey Campaigns

Surveys are a powerful tool for gathering feedback, understanding customer needs, and improving your offerings. WhatsApp's interactive nature makes it an ideal platform for conducting surveys and collecting insights directly from your audience.

- **Customer Satisfaction Surveys**: After a purchase or interaction with your brand, sending a customer satisfaction survey via WhatsApp allows you to quickly gather feedback on the customer experience. These surveys can be simple and direct, asking for ratings on specific aspects of your service, or more detailed, exploring various elements of the customer journey. The immediacy of WhatsApp increases the likelihood of receiving timely and honest feedback.

- **Market Research Surveys**: Use WhatsApp to conduct market research by sending surveys that explore customer preferences, needs, and opinions on potential new products or services. By engaging your audience in this way, you can gain valuable insights that inform your product development and marketing strategies. For instance, you could ask your contacts which features they'd like to see in a future product, helping you align your offerings with customer expectations.

- **Feedback on Specific Campaigns**: After running a promotion or event, use WhatsApp to gather feedback on how it was received. Asking your audience what they liked, what could be improved, or whether they would participate in similar events in the future provides actionable insights that can be used to refine your strategies. This type of survey not only helps improve future campaigns but also demonstrates that you value your customers' opinions.

- **Interactive Polls and Quizzes**: Engage your audience with interactive polls or quizzes that allow them to share their preferences or opinions in real time. WhatsApp's polling feature is a quick and easy way to gather input on a specific topic, such as which product color they prefer or what type of content they want to see more of. This not only provides valuable data but also encourages active participation and strengthens your connection with your audience.

WhatsApp offers a dynamic platform for running a wide range of marketing campaigns, from promotions and announcements to surveys. Each type of campaign serves a unique purpose and can be tailored to meet specific business objectives. By understanding the different types of campaigns and how to execute them effectively, you can harness the full potential of WhatsApp as a marketing tool, driving engagement, building relationships, and achieving measurable results. In the next section, we will explore the process of executing these campaigns, from planning to analysis, ensuring you can optimize your efforts for maximum impact.

6.2 Timing Your Messages for Maximum Impact

Timing is a crucial element in the success of any marketing campaign, and WhatsApp is no exception. Given the personal and direct nature of the platform, sending your messages at the right time can significantly enhance engagement, drive higher response rates, and ultimately contribute to the success of your campaign. In this section, we will explore the strategies and considerations for timing your WhatsApp messages to maximize their impact.

Understanding Your Audience's Behavior

The foundation of effective message timing lies in understanding your audience's behavior and routines. This involves knowing when they are most likely to be online, available to read messages, and in a mindset to engage with your content. Analyzing your audience's behavior through previous engagement data, social media activity, and even general market research can provide insights into their daily patterns.

- **Daily Routines**: People tend to have consistent daily routines that influence when they check their messages. For example, many users are more likely to engage with WhatsApp during their morning commute, lunch break, or after work hours.

Understanding these routines can help you schedule your messages for times when your audience is most receptive.

- **Time Zones**: If your audience is spread across different regions, it's important to consider time zones when scheduling your messages. Sending a message at a time that is convenient for one segment of your audience may be ineffective for another. Segmenting your audience by time zone and scheduling messages accordingly can help ensure that your content reaches everyone at an optimal time.
- **Weekdays vs. Weekends**: Engagement patterns often vary between weekdays and weekends. During weekdays, people might be more responsive during work breaks or in the evening, whereas weekends may see higher engagement during midday or early afternoon. Testing different times across various days of the week can help you identify the best times to reach your audience.

Leveraging Data and Analytics

Data-driven decision-making is key to optimizing the timing of your WhatsApp messages. By analyzing past campaign performance, you can identify patterns and trends that inform your timing strategy.

- **Engagement Metrics**: Analyze metrics such as open rates, response rates, and click-through rates to determine when your messages have historically performed best. Look for patterns that indicate peak engagement times, and use this data to inform future message scheduling.
- **A/B Testing**: Conduct A/B testing by sending the same message at different times to segments of your audience. Compare the results to see which timing yields the highest engagement. Over time,

these tests can help you refine your timing strategy to maximize impact.

- **Feedback Loops**: Continuously gather and analyze feedback from your campaigns to adjust your timing strategy. If you notice a drop in engagement at certain times, experiment with different schedules until you find the optimal timing for your messages.

Considering the Nature of Your Message

The content and purpose of your message should also influence its timing. Different types of messages may be more effective at certain times of the day or week, depending on their nature and the desired outcome.

- **Promotional Messages**: Promotions that require immediate action, such as flash sales or limited-time offers, should be sent at times when your audience is most likely to be active and ready to make a purchase. This could be during peak shopping hours or when they are most likely to have free time to browse and buy.
- **Informational Updates**: Announcements or informational messages that don't require immediate action can be sent during off-peak times when your message is less likely to compete with others. For example, sending an update during mid-morning or mid-afternoon can ensure it is noticed without being lost in the morning rush.
- **Surveys and Feedback Requests**: If you're seeking feedback or conducting a survey, timing is crucial to ensure that recipients have the time and focus to respond thoughtfully. Sending these messages during the evening or on weekends, when people are more relaxed, can lead to higher participation rates.

Taking Advantage of WhatsApp Features

WhatsApp offers several features that can help you optimize the timing and delivery of your messages. Understanding and utilizing these features can enhance the effectiveness of your timing strategy.

- **Scheduled Messages**: While WhatsApp itself does not offer a built-in message scheduling feature, third-party tools and integrations can enable you to schedule messages for future delivery. This is particularly useful for automating campaigns that need to go out at specific times or across different time zones.
- **Broadcast Lists**: Broadcast lists allow you to send messages to multiple recipients simultaneously, while still delivering them as individual messages. This ensures that your timing is consistent across your audience, and messages are more likely to be read and responded to quickly.
- **WhatsApp Status**: For campaigns that don't require direct messaging, using WhatsApp Status can be an effective way to share time-sensitive updates or promotions. Since Status updates disappear after 24 hours, they create a sense of urgency and can be timed to coincide with peak activity periods.

Balancing Frequency and Timing

While timing is critical, it must be balanced with frequency to avoid overwhelming your audience. Sending messages too frequently, even at optimal times, can lead to message fatigue and disengagement.

- **Message Cadence**: Establish a message cadence that balances regular communication with giving your audience enough time between messages. For example, daily messages may be appropriate for a short-term campaign or event countdown, while weekly messages may be better for ongoing engagement.
- **Avoiding Spamming**: Be mindful of not overwhelming your audience with too many messages, especially if they are sent at inopportune times. Excessive messaging can lead to higher opt-out rates and reduced engagement.
- **Listening to Your Audience**: Pay attention to feedback from your audience regarding the frequency and timing of your messages. If you receive complaints or notice a drop in engagement, it may be a sign that you need to adjust your approach.

Timing your WhatsApp messages for maximum impact requires a combination of audience insights, data analysis, and strategic planning. By understanding when your audience is most likely to engage, leveraging the right tools and features, and carefully balancing frequency and timing, you can enhance the effectiveness of your WhatsApp campaigns. This strategic approach ensures that your messages are not only seen but also acted upon, driving better results and a stronger connection with your audience. In the following sections, we will delve into advanced techniques for optimizing your WhatsApp campaigns and integrating them with your broader marketing efforts.

6.3 A/B Testing and Analyzing Campaign Performance

In the dynamic world of WhatsApp marketing, A/B testing and performance analysis are indispensable tools for optimizing your campaigns. By systematically comparing different approaches and measuring outcomes, you can refine your strategies, improve engagement, and maximize the effectiveness of your marketing efforts. In this section, we'll explore how to conduct A/B testing on WhatsApp and analyze campaign performance to drive continuous improvement.

Understanding A/B Testing

A/B testing, also known as split testing, involves creating two or more versions of a message or campaign element to determine which performs better. The goal is to identify the most effective approach by comparing key metrics such as open rates, click-through rates, conversion rates, and engagement levels.

- **Choosing Variables to Test**: The first step in A/B testing is deciding which elements of your WhatsApp campaign you want to test. Common variables include the message content (e.g., text, images, call-to-action), timing, audience segmentation, and message format. For example, you might test two different headlines to see which one generates more clicks or compare two types of media (images vs. videos) to determine which drives higher engagement.
- **Creating Test Groups**: Once you've identified the variables to test, divide your audience into separate groups that will each receive a different version of the message. It's important to ensure that these groups are similar in size and composition to obtain reliable results. For example, if you're testing a promotional message, you might split your audience into two equal segments, with each group receiving a different version of the promotion.
- **Running the Test**: After setting up your test groups, send out the different versions of your message simultaneously to minimize the

impact of external factors such as time of day or day of the week. It's crucial to monitor the test closely to ensure that everything is running smoothly and to make any necessary adjustments in real time.

- **Measuring Results**: Once the test is complete, compare the performance of each version by analyzing key metrics. For instance, you might compare the open rates, click-through rates, or conversion rates between the two groups to determine which version was more successful. The version with the higher performance is typically the one you'll want to implement on a larger scale.

Key Metrics for Campaign Performance Analysis

Analyzing the performance of your WhatsApp campaigns involves tracking a variety of metrics that provide insights into how well your campaigns are performing and where there is room for improvement.

- **Open Rate**: The open rate measures the percentage of recipients who opened your message. A high open rate indicates that your message was compelling enough to prompt recipients to read it, while a low open rate may suggest that the message was not relevant or was sent at an inopportune time.
- **Click-Through Rate (CTR)**: The CTR measures the percentage of recipients who clicked on a link or call to action within your message. This metric is crucial for evaluating the effectiveness of your content and the strength of your call to action. A high CTR indicates that your message resonated with your audience and motivated them to take action.

- **Conversion Rate**: The conversion rate measures the percentage of recipients who completed the desired action, such as making a purchase or signing up for a newsletter, after clicking through from your WhatsApp message. This metric is key to assessing the overall success of your campaign in achieving its objectives.
- **Engagement Rate**: The engagement rate encompasses various forms of interaction with your message, including responses, shares, and media views. High engagement indicates that your content was well-received and sparked meaningful interactions with your audience.
- **Opt-Out Rate**: The opt-out rate measures the percentage of recipients who unsubscribed from your WhatsApp messages after receiving a campaign. A high opt-out rate can be a red flag, indicating that your messaging frequency, content, or relevance may need to be reassessed.
- **Response Time**: Response time tracks how quickly your audience engages with your message after it's been sent. Faster response times generally indicate a higher level of interest and relevance.

Interpreting A/B Testing Results

Interpreting the results of your A/B tests requires a combination of quantitative analysis and qualitative insights. It's not just about which version performed better, but also about understanding why one version was more successful than the other.

- **Statistical Significance**: Ensure that the differences in performance between your test versions are statistically significant. This means that the results are not due to random chance but are a true reflection of how each version performs. Statistical tools can help you determine whether your results are significant.

- **Identifying Patterns**: Look for patterns in your A/B testing results that might provide broader insights into your audience's preferences. For example, if you consistently see higher engagement with messages sent in the evening, this could inform the timing of future campaigns across the board.
- **Qualitative Feedback**: In addition to quantitative metrics, consider any qualitative feedback you receive from your audience during the test. This might include direct responses to your messages or trends in customer inquiries. This feedback can provide valuable context to your quantitative data and help you understand the "why" behind the results.

Continuous Improvement through Performance Analysis

Performance analysis is not a one-time task but an ongoing process that should be integrated into your overall marketing strategy. By regularly analyzing the results of your WhatsApp campaigns, you can continuously refine your approach, improve engagement, and achieve better results over time.

- **Iterative Testing**: A/B testing should be an iterative process. After implementing the winning version of your test, consider testing additional variables to further optimize your campaign. For example, after identifying the most effective message content, you might test different timing or audience segments to maximize impact.
- **Benchmarking**: Establish benchmarks for your key metrics based on past performance. These benchmarks can serve as reference

points for evaluating the success of future campaigns. If a new campaign performs above your established benchmarks, it's a strong indicator that your strategy is working well.

- **Learning from Failures**: Not all A/B tests will yield positive results, and that's okay. Sometimes, a test may show that a new approach is less effective than your existing strategy. Use these failures as learning opportunities to refine your understanding of your audience and improve future campaigns.
- **Integrating Insights**: The insights gained from your A/B testing and performance analysis should be integrated into your broader marketing strategy. This might involve adjusting your messaging, refining your targeting, or rethinking your content strategy to better align with what resonates with your audience on WhatsApp.

A/B testing and performance analysis are powerful tools for optimizing your WhatsApp marketing campaigns. By systematically testing different approaches and analyzing key metrics, you can gain valuable insights into what works best for your audience. This data-driven approach allows you to refine your strategies, enhance engagement, and achieve better results over time. In the next sections, we'll explore advanced techniques for leveraging WhatsApp's features to further boost your campaign performance and drive success in your marketing efforts.

6.4 Tools and Software for WhatsApp Campaign Management

Managing WhatsApp marketing campaigns effectively requires the use of specialized tools and software that streamline operations, enhance communication, and provide valuable insights. With the right tools, you can automate processes, track performance, and optimize your campaigns for better results. In this section, we'll explore some of the most useful tools and software available for WhatsApp campaign management, along with their key features and benefits.

WhatsApp Business API

The WhatsApp Business API is a powerful tool designed for medium to large businesses looking to engage with customers at scale. Unlike the WhatsApp Business App, which is intended for small businesses, the API offers extensive functionality for automation, integration, and analytics.

- **Automation and Integration**: The WhatsApp Business API allows you to automate customer interactions through chatbots, which can handle everything from answering FAQs to processing orders. It also integrates seamlessly with customer relationship management (CRM) systems, marketing automation platforms, and other business tools, enabling a unified approach to customer communication.
- **Personalization at Scale**: The API supports personalized messaging, allowing you to tailor content based on customer data. This enhances the relevance of your messages and can lead to higher engagement and conversion rates.
- **Security and Compliance**: The API offers robust security features, including end-to-end encryption, which ensures that customer data is protected. Additionally, it helps businesses comply with regulations like GDPR by offering tools to manage consent and data privacy.

- **Detailed Analytics**: With the WhatsApp Business API, you can track a wide range of metrics, including message delivery rates, read receipts, and response times. This data is crucial for optimizing your campaigns and improving customer interactions.

Chatbot Platforms

Chatbots are essential for automating customer interactions on WhatsApp, and several platforms offer sophisticated chatbot development and management tools. These platforms allow businesses to create, deploy, and manage chatbots without needing extensive technical expertise.

- **Chatfuel**: Originally designed for Facebook Messenger, Chatfuel now offers integration with WhatsApp through third-party services. It allows you to build bots using a visual interface, making it easy to create complex conversational flows. Chatfuel also supports AI-driven interactions, enabling more natural conversations with customers.
- **ManyChat**: Like Chatfuel, ManyChat is a popular chatbot platform that has expanded to support WhatsApp. It offers a drag-and-drop interface for building bots, along with tools for segmenting your audience, sending broadcasts, and analyzing performance. ManyChat's integration with WhatsApp makes it easier to manage cross-platform campaigns.
- **Twilio**: Twilio offers a robust API for building and managing chatbots on WhatsApp. It provides advanced features like natural language processing (NLP) and AI-powered interactions, which allow for more sophisticated customer engagement. Twilio also

integrates with other communication channels, enabling a cohesive omnichannel strategy.

Customer Relationship Management (CRM) Systems

Integrating WhatsApp with your CRM system allows you to manage customer interactions more effectively, track customer data, and personalize communications. This integration is particularly valuable for businesses that rely on detailed customer insights to drive marketing strategies.

- **HubSpot**: HubSpot is a leading CRM platform that offers WhatsApp integration through third-party tools. This integration allows you to track conversations, manage contacts, and automate follow-up messages. HubSpot also offers powerful analytics tools, helping you measure the impact of your WhatsApp campaigns on customer relationships.
- **Salesforce**: Salesforce is another top CRM platform that supports WhatsApp integration. With Salesforce, you can manage all customer interactions from a single platform, ensuring consistency across all communication channels. Salesforce's AI-driven analytics provide deep insights into customer behavior, which can be used to optimize your WhatsApp marketing efforts.
- **Zoho CRM**: Zoho CRM is a cost-effective solution for small to medium-sized businesses. It offers WhatsApp integration through its omnichannel platform, allowing you to manage WhatsApp conversations alongside emails, social media messages, and other communications. Zoho CRM also offers automation tools for streamlining customer interactions.

Marketing Automation Tools

Marketing automation tools help you manage WhatsApp campaigns more efficiently by automating repetitive tasks, segmenting your audience, and delivering personalized messages at scale. These tools are essential for businesses looking to optimize their marketing efforts across multiple channels.

- **ActiveCampaign**: ActiveCampaign offers WhatsApp integration as part of its broader marketing automation platform. This integration allows you to create automated workflows that trigger WhatsApp messages based on customer behavior, such as cart abandonment or lead scoring. ActiveCampaign's detailed reporting tools provide insights into the performance of your WhatsApp campaigns.
- **MoEngage**: MoEngage is a customer engagement platform that supports WhatsApp messaging as part of its omnichannel marketing capabilities. It allows you to segment your audience, personalize messages, and automate campaigns based on customer actions. MoEngage also provides advanced analytics for measuring campaign performance across all channels.
- **Sendinblue**: Sendinblue offers WhatsApp integration through its automation platform, enabling businesses to send targeted messages, manage customer interactions, and track performance. Sendinblue is particularly well-suited for small businesses looking for an affordable marketing automation solution with WhatsApp capabilities.

Analytics and Reporting Tools

To optimize your WhatsApp campaigns, it's crucial to analyze performance data and gain insights into customer behavior. Several tools offer advanced analytics and reporting features that help you track key metrics, identify trends, and make data-driven decisions.

- **Google Analytics**: While Google Analytics is not directly integrated with WhatsApp, it can be used to track traffic and conversions from WhatsApp campaigns. By creating custom UTM parameters for your WhatsApp links, you can monitor how much traffic is being driven to your website and measure the impact of your WhatsApp marketing efforts.
- **WATI**: WATI (WhatsApp Team Inbox) is a tool specifically designed for WhatsApp Business API users. It provides detailed analytics and reporting features, including metrics on message delivery, open rates, and response times. WATI's analytics dashboard offers a comprehensive view of your WhatsApp campaign performance.
- **Clickatell**: Clickatell is a messaging platform that provides robust analytics for WhatsApp campaigns. It allows you to track delivery and read rates, measure engagement, and analyze customer interactions. Clickatell's analytics tools help businesses optimize their messaging strategy and improve customer engagement.

Scheduling and Automation Tools

Scheduling tools are essential for planning and automating the delivery of WhatsApp messages, ensuring that your campaigns reach the right audience at the right time. These tools also help you manage message frequency and avoid overwhelming your audience.

- **Buffer**: Although Buffer is primarily known for social media scheduling, it also offers WhatsApp integration through third-party services. Buffer allows you to schedule WhatsApp messages in advance, ensuring timely delivery of your campaigns. This is particularly useful for managing content across multiple channels.
- **Hootsuite**: Hootsuite is another popular social media management tool that supports WhatsApp scheduling through integrations. With Hootsuite, you can plan and automate WhatsApp campaigns alongside your social media strategy, maintaining consistency across all platforms.
- **WhatsApp Scheduler Tools**: Several tools specifically designed for WhatsApp scheduling are available, such as WhatsApp Scheduler or Scheduler Bot. These tools allow you to schedule messages, set reminders, and automate follow-ups, making it easier to manage your campaigns effectively.

Effective WhatsApp campaign management requires the use of specialized tools and software that streamline processes, automate tasks, and provide valuable insights. From chatbots and CRM systems to marketing automation platforms and analytics tools, the right combination of technology can significantly enhance the effectiveness of your WhatsApp marketing efforts. By leveraging these tools, businesses can not only improve their campaign performance but also create more personalized and engaging experiences for their customers. In the following chapters, we'll explore how to put these tools into practice and integrate them into your overall marketing strategy for maximum impact.

Chapter 7: Measuring Success: Analytics and KPIs

In the world of WhatsApp marketing, success isn't just about the number of messages sent or the size of your contact list; it's about how effectively your campaigns achieve their objectives. To understand the impact of your efforts and make data-driven decisions, you need to measure key performance indicators (KPIs) and analyze the results of your campaigns. This chapter delves into the essential metrics and tools for tracking the success of your WhatsApp marketing initiatives.

1. The Importance of Measuring Success

Measuring the success of your WhatsApp marketing campaigns is crucial for several reasons. First, it allows you to determine whether your strategies are working as intended and delivering the desired outcomes. Without measurement, you're essentially operating in the dark, unable to assess the effectiveness of your efforts. Second, analyzing KPIs helps you identify areas for improvement, enabling you to refine your approach and optimize future campaigns. Lastly, data-driven insights provide a solid foundation for justifying your marketing spend and demonstrating the value of your WhatsApp marketing efforts to stakeholders.

2. Key Performance Indicators (KPIs) for WhatsApp Marketing

KPIs are specific metrics that help you gauge the effectiveness of your WhatsApp marketing campaigns. The right KPIs will depend on your business goals, but the following are some of the most commonly used metrics in WhatsApp marketing:

- **Message Delivery Rate**: The percentage of messages successfully delivered to your audience. A high delivery rate indicates that your contact list is up-to-date and that your messages are reaching their intended recipients.
- **Message Open Rate**: The percentage of delivered messages that are opened by recipients. This metric is a strong indicator of the relevance and timing of your messages. High open rates suggest that your content is resonating with your audience, while low open rates may signal a need to improve your messaging strategy.
- **Click-Through Rate (CTR)**: The percentage of recipients who click on a link or call to action within your message. CTR is a key indicator of engagement and the effectiveness of your content. A high CTR means your audience is interested in what you have to offer, whereas a low CTR may suggest that your call-to-action needs improvement.
- **Conversion Rate**: The percentage of recipients who take the desired action after clicking through your message, such as making a purchase or signing up for a newsletter. Conversion rate is a critical KPI that directly ties your WhatsApp marketing efforts to business outcomes.
- **Engagement Rate**: This metric measures the level of interaction with your messages, including responses, shares, and media views. A high engagement rate indicates that your audience finds your content valuable and is willing to engage with it.
- **Response Time**: The average time it takes for recipients to respond to your messages. Faster response times generally indicate higher interest and relevance of your content, while longer

response times may suggest a need to improve your message timing or content.

- **Opt-Out Rate**: The percentage of recipients who unsubscribe from your WhatsApp messages after receiving a campaign. A high opt-out rate can be a red flag, indicating that your messaging frequency, content, or relevance needs to be reassessed.
- **Customer Satisfaction (CSAT) Score**: A measure of how satisfied your customers are with their interactions with your business on WhatsApp. This can be gathered through follow-up surveys or direct feedback after customer service interactions.

3. Tools for Tracking and Analyzing WhatsApp Marketing Performance

To effectively measure the success of your WhatsApp marketing campaigns, you need the right tools to track and analyze your KPIs. Here are some of the most effective tools for WhatsApp marketing analytics:

- **Google Analytics**: While Google Analytics is primarily used for tracking website performance, it can also be utilized to monitor the traffic and conversions driven by your WhatsApp campaigns. By creating UTM parameters for your WhatsApp links, you can track how much traffic your website receives from WhatsApp and measure the effectiveness of your campaigns.
- **WhatsApp Business API Dashboard**: For businesses using the WhatsApp Business API, the built-in analytics dashboard provides a wealth of data on message delivery rates, open rates, response times, and more. This data is crucial for monitoring the performance of your campaigns and making data-driven decisions.

- **WATI (WhatsApp Team Inbox)**: WATI is a specialized tool for businesses using the WhatsApp Business API. It offers advanced analytics features, including metrics on message delivery, read receipts, and response times. WATI's analytics dashboard provides a comprehensive view of your WhatsApp campaign performance, helping you identify trends and optimize your strategy.
- **Clickatell**: Clickatell is a messaging platform that provides detailed analytics for WhatsApp campaigns. It allows you to track delivery and read rates, measure engagement, and analyze customer interactions. Clickatell's analytics tools are designed to help businesses optimize their messaging strategy and improve customer engagement.
- **HubSpot**: HubSpot's CRM platform integrates with WhatsApp and offers robust analytics tools for tracking customer interactions, managing contacts, and automating follow-up messages. HubSpot's detailed reporting features provide insights into the impact of your WhatsApp campaigns on customer relationships.

4. Setting Benchmarks and Goals

Setting benchmarks and goals is an essential step in measuring the success of your WhatsApp marketing efforts. Benchmarks provide a point of reference for evaluating the performance of your campaigns, while goals give you a clear target to aim for. Here's how to set effective benchmarks and goals:

- **Establish Baseline Metrics**: Before launching a new campaign, it's important to establish baseline metrics based on your past performance. These metrics will serve as a benchmark for evaluating the success of your new campaigns. For example, if your average CTR for previous campaigns was 5%, this can serve as a benchmark for future efforts.

- **Set SMART Goals**: Your marketing goals should be Specific, Measurable, Achievable, Relevant, and Time-bound (SMART). For instance, instead of setting a vague goal like "increase engagement," you might set a SMART goal like "increase the click-through rate by 10% over the next three months."

- **Monitor Progress Regularly**: Regularly monitoring your progress towards your goals is crucial for ensuring that you stay on track. Use your analytics tools to track your KPIs and compare them against your benchmarks and goals. If you're not meeting your targets, analyze the data to identify potential issues and adjust your strategy accordingly.

- **Adjust Goals as Needed**: As you gather more data and insights from your campaigns, you may need to adjust your goals. For example, if you consistently exceed your CTR goal, you might set a more ambitious target. Conversely, if you're struggling to meet your goals, consider adjusting them to be more realistic based on your performance data.

5. Interpreting Data and Making Data-Driven Decisions

Collecting data is only the first step; the real value lies in interpreting that data and using it to make informed decisions. Here's how to effectively interpret your WhatsApp marketing data and apply it to your strategy:

- **Look for Patterns and Trends**: Analyze your data to identify patterns and trends that can inform your marketing strategy. For example, if you notice that your messages tend to receive higher open rates in the evenings, consider scheduling future campaigns for that time.

- **Compare Performance Across Campaigns**: Comparing the performance of different campaigns can provide valuable insights into what works and what doesn't. For example, if one campaign outperforms another, try to identify the factors that contributed to its success, such as the message content, timing, or audience segment.

- **Conduct A/B Testing**: A/B testing, as discussed in a previous chapter, is a powerful tool for optimizing your campaigns. Use your data to test different variables, such as message content or timing, and analyze the results to determine the most effective approach.

- **Use Data to Optimize Campaigns**: The ultimate goal of analyzing your WhatsApp marketing data is to optimize your campaigns for better results. Use the insights you gain from your data to refine your messaging, targeting, and overall strategy. For example, if your data shows that personalized messages have higher engagement rates, consider incorporating more personalization into your future campaigns.

- **Report Findings to Stakeholders**: If you're responsible for reporting the success of your WhatsApp marketing efforts to stakeholders, use your data to provide clear, actionable insights. Present your findings in a way that demonstrates the value of your campaigns and highlights areas for improvement.

Measuring success in WhatsApp marketing is about more than just tracking metrics; it's about using data to drive continuous improvement. By focusing on key performance indicators, leveraging the right tools, setting benchmarks and goals, and making data-driven decisions, you can optimize your WhatsApp marketing strategy and achieve better results over time. In the next chapter, we'll explore advanced techniques for scaling your WhatsApp marketing efforts and integrating them into your broader digital marketing strategy.

7.1 Key Metrics for WhatsApp Marketing

To evaluate the effectiveness of your WhatsApp marketing campaigns, it's essential to track specific metrics that provide insight into how well your messages are resonating with your audience and achieving your business objectives. The following key metrics are critical for understanding the performance of your WhatsApp marketing efforts:

Message Delivery Rate

The message delivery rate measures the percentage of messages successfully delivered to your recipients. This metric is a fundamental indicator of your campaign's reach and the accuracy of your contact list. A high delivery rate suggests that your contact database is well-maintained and that your messages are reaching their intended audience. Conversely, a low delivery rate might indicate issues such as outdated contact information or technical problems with message transmission.

Message Open Rate

The message open rate represents the percentage of delivered messages that are opened by recipients. This metric is crucial for assessing the initial effectiveness of your campaign. High open rates indicate that your subject lines, previews, or message timing are compelling enough to encourage recipients to open the message. Low open rates, on the other hand, may suggest that your content isn't capturing your audience's attention or that your messages are being sent at less optimal times.

Click-Through Rate (CTR)

The click-through rate (CTR) measures the percentage of recipients who click on a link, button, or call-to-action (CTA) within your message. This metric provides insight into how engaging and relevant your content is. A high CTR indicates that your audience finds your message compelling enough to take the desired action, whether that's visiting a website, making a purchase, or signing up for a service. If your CTR is low, you might need to re-evaluate your CTA, the relevance of your content, or the placement of links within the message.

Conversion Rate

The conversion rate is one of the most critical metrics, as it measures the percentage of recipients who complete the desired action after clicking through your message. This could be making a purchase, filling out a form, or any other action that aligns with your campaign goals. The conversion rate directly ties your WhatsApp marketing efforts to tangible business outcomes, making it a key indicator of your campaign's overall success. Improving your conversion rate often involves optimizing the user experience on the landing page, ensuring the relevance of your offers, and refining your CTA.

Engagement Rate

The engagement rate measures the level of interaction with your WhatsApp messages beyond just opening them. This can include actions such as replies, shares, or viewing attached media like images or videos. High engagement rates indicate that your content resonates with your audience and encourages interaction. Engagement is particularly important in building relationships and maintaining ongoing communication with your customers.

Response Time

Response time tracks how quickly recipients respond to your messages. This metric is especially relevant for customer service interactions on WhatsApp, where timely responses can significantly impact customer satisfaction. Shorter response times generally reflect positively on your brand, demonstrating responsiveness and attentiveness to customer needs.

Opt-Out Rate

The opt-out rate measures the percentage of recipients who choose to unsubscribe from your WhatsApp messages after receiving a campaign. This metric is important for understanding how your audience perceives the frequency and relevance of your messages. A high opt-out rate may indicate that your messages are too frequent, irrelevant, or not aligned with your audience's preferences. Monitoring and analyzing opt-out rates can help you adjust your messaging strategy to better meet your audience's expectations.

Customer Satisfaction (CSAT) Score

The Customer Satisfaction (CSAT) score is a measure of how satisfied your customers are with their interactions with your brand on WhatsApp. This score is typically gathered through follow-up surveys or direct feedback after customer service interactions. A high CSAT score indicates that your WhatsApp communication is meeting or exceeding customer expectations, while a low score may signal areas where improvement is needed, such as response time, message clarity, or the quality of support provided.

Cost Per Message/Cost Per Acquisition

For businesses concerned with the financial efficiency of their campaigns, tracking the cost per message sent and the cost per acquisition (CPA) is essential. These metrics help you understand the economic impact of your WhatsApp marketing efforts. By comparing these costs against the revenue generated from conversions, you can evaluate the return on investment (ROI) for your campaigns. Lowering your CPA while maintaining or increasing conversion rates is a sign of a highly effective campaign.

Tracking and analyzing these key metrics will provide you with a comprehensive understanding of how your WhatsApp marketing campaigns are performing. By focusing on metrics such as delivery and open rates, CTR, conversion rates, and customer satisfaction, you can make data-driven decisions to optimize your campaigns, enhance customer engagement, and ultimately achieve better business outcomes. As you continue to refine your approach, these metrics will serve as valuable indicators of your progress and success.

7.2 Tracking Engagement, Conversion Rates, and ROI

In WhatsApp marketing, understanding how well your campaigns resonate with your audience and contribute to your business objectives is crucial. Tracking engagement, conversion rates, and return on investment (ROI) provides valuable insights into the effectiveness of your efforts. These metrics help you determine what's working, identify areas for improvement, and optimize your strategy for better results.

Tracking Engagement

Engagement is a key indicator of how your audience interacts with your content. It goes beyond just message delivery and open rates, focusing on the depth of interaction your messages receive. Tracking engagement on WhatsApp involves monitoring several aspects of how your audience responds to your content:

- **Message Responses**: One of the most direct indicators of engagement is how often recipients reply to your messages. High response rates suggest that your content is relevant and prompts interaction. Tracking these responses can help you understand what types of content resonate best with your audience.
- **Content Interaction**: Engagement also includes how recipients interact with the content within your messages, such as watching

videos, viewing images, or clicking on links. Monitoring these interactions gives you insight into which types of media and content formats are most effective at capturing attention and encouraging further engagement.

- **Shares and Forwards**: If your content is being shared or forwarded by recipients to others, it's a strong sign of high engagement. This indicates that your messages are not only valuable to your initial audience but also to a broader group, amplifying your reach organically.
- **Group Participation**: If you're using WhatsApp groups as part of your marketing strategy, tracking the level of participation within these groups is crucial. Active discussions, frequent message exchanges, and regular interactions are signs of a highly engaged audience.

Understanding engagement trends can guide your content strategy, helping you create messages that are more likely to resonate with your audience and prompt meaningful interactions.

Tracking Conversion Rates

Conversion rate is a critical metric that directly ties your WhatsApp marketing efforts to your business objectives. It measures the percentage of recipients who take a desired action after interacting with your message, such as making a purchase, signing up for a service, or downloading a resource.

- **Defining Conversions**: The first step in tracking conversion rates is to clearly define what constitutes a conversion for your campaign. This could vary depending on your specific goals, such as product sales, lead generation, or customer registration.

- **Setting Up Conversion Tracking**: To track conversions effectively, you need to set up tracking mechanisms that link actions taken on WhatsApp to your conversion goals. This might involve using tracking links (with UTM parameters) that direct recipients to a specific landing page where their actions can be recorded. For more advanced campaigns, integrating WhatsApp with CRM or e-commerce platforms can provide deeper insights into conversion behavior.
- **Analyzing Conversion Data**: Once conversions are tracked, analyzing the data can reveal which messages, content types, and campaigns are most effective at driving desired actions. You can segment conversion data by factors like audience demographics, time of day, and message type to identify trends and optimize future campaigns.
- **Improving Conversion Rates**: Based on your analysis, you can experiment with different strategies to improve conversion rates. This might include refining your call-to-action (CTA), adjusting the timing of your messages, or personalizing content to better align with audience interests.

Tracking Return on Investment (ROI)

Return on investment (ROI) is perhaps the most critical metric for determining the financial effectiveness of your WhatsApp marketing campaigns. ROI measures the revenue generated from your campaigns relative to the costs incurred, providing a clear picture of whether your efforts are yielding profitable results.

Calculating ROI: ROI is typically calculated using the following formula:

$$\text{ROI} = \frac{\text{Revenue from Campaign} - \text{Cost of Campaign}}{\text{Cost of Campaign}} \times 100$$

To calculate ROI accurately, you need to account for all costs associated with your campaign, including the cost of content creation, message distribution, and any tools or software used for campaign management. The revenue generated can be tracked through sales data, lead conversions, or other relevant financial metrics.

- **Attributing Revenue**: One of the challenges in calculating ROI is accurately attributing revenue to your WhatsApp campaigns, especially if your marketing efforts span multiple channels. Using unique tracking links, coupon codes, or tracking integrations with your sales platform can help attribute sales and revenue directly to your WhatsApp marketing efforts.
- **Analyzing ROI**: Once you've calculated ROI, analyze the results to understand the financial impact of your campaigns. A positive ROI indicates that your campaign is profitable, while a negative ROI suggests that the costs outweigh the revenue generated. This analysis can help you determine which campaigns are worth scaling and which ones need adjustments or reevaluation.
- **Improving ROI**: To improve ROI, focus on optimizing both sides of the equation—reducing campaign costs and increasing revenue. This could involve refining your targeting to reach more high-value customers, enhancing the effectiveness of your messaging, or automating parts of your campaign to reduce operational costs.

Tracking engagement, conversion rates, and ROI is essential for understanding the impact of your WhatsApp marketing efforts and making data-driven decisions. By closely monitoring these metrics, you can identify successful strategies, optimize underperforming campaigns, and ensure that your WhatsApp marketing contributes meaningfully to your business objectives. As you refine your approach based on these insights, you'll be better positioned to achieve sustained success in your WhatsApp marketing initiatives.

7.3 Adjusting Your Strategy Based on Analytics

In the fast-paced world of digital marketing, continuous improvement is key to staying competitive. Analyzing the data from your WhatsApp marketing campaigns provides a wealth of information that can guide strategic adjustments, ensuring that your efforts are both effective and aligned with your business goals. This section will explore how to use analytics to refine your WhatsApp marketing strategy, improve performance, and maximize your return on investment.

Identifying Strengths and Weaknesses

The first step in adjusting your strategy is to identify what's working well and what isn't. By closely examining key metrics such as engagement rates, conversion rates, and ROI, you can pinpoint areas of success and areas that need improvement.

- **Analyzing High-Performing Content**: Review the content that has the highest engagement and conversion rates. Identify patterns in the type of content, messaging tone, timing, and format. For instance, if video messages consistently yield higher engagement, it might be beneficial to incorporate more video content into your strategy.

- **Spotting Underperforming Areas**: Conversely, analyze the campaigns or messages that didn't meet expectations. Look for common factors that might have contributed to lower performance, such as the time of day messages were sent, the relevance of the content, or the clarity of the call-to-action. Understanding these shortcomings allows you to avoid repeating the same mistakes in future campaigns.

Refining Audience Targeting

One of the most impactful ways to adjust your strategy is by refining your audience targeting based on analytics. Effective targeting ensures that your messages reach the right people, increasing the likelihood of engagement and conversion.

- **Segmenting Your Audience**: Use analytics to segment your audience into smaller, more specific groups based on factors like demographics, behavior, or past interactions. For example, you might identify a segment of your audience that responds well to promotional offers, while another segment is more interested in educational content. Tailoring your messages to these segments can significantly improve your campaign's effectiveness.
- **Personalizing Content**: Personalized content resonates more with recipients, leading to higher engagement and conversion rates. By analyzing past campaign data, you can gain insights into individual preferences and behaviors, allowing you to craft more personalized

and relevant messages. For instance, if a particular segment frequently clicks on content related to a specific product, you can send targeted promotions for that product to those users.

Optimizing Message Timing and Frequency

The timing and frequency of your messages play a crucial role in their effectiveness. Analytics can provide insights into the optimal times to send messages and how often you should communicate with your audience.

- **Timing Analysis**: Review the times when your messages received the highest open and engagement rates. This data can help you identify the best times to send future messages. For example, if your audience tends to engage more with your content in the late afternoon, adjust your message schedule accordingly.
- **Balancing Frequency**: While frequent communication can keep your brand top-of-mind, over-communicating can lead to audience fatigue and higher opt-out rates. Use analytics to find the right balance, ensuring that you stay connected with your audience without overwhelming them. Monitoring metrics like engagement rates and opt-out rates over time can help you adjust the frequency of your messages.

Improving Conversion Paths

Analytics can shed light on the effectiveness of your conversion paths— the steps your audience takes from receiving a message to completing a desired action. By analyzing where users drop off in the process, you can make strategic adjustments to improve conversion rates.

- **Streamlining the User Journey**: If analytics reveal that many users are abandoning the conversion process at a particular stage, it may indicate friction in the user journey. Simplify the process by reducing the number of steps required to complete an action, ensuring that landing pages are user-friendly, and optimizing the overall experience.
- **Enhancing Call-to-Action (CTA)**: The effectiveness of your CTA can make or break a campaign. Use data to assess which CTAs are most successful at driving conversions. Experiment with different wording, placements, and formats to find the most compelling CTAs for your audience.

Testing and Iterating

Continuous testing and iteration are essential for refining your WhatsApp marketing strategy. Use the insights gained from analytics to conduct A/B testing, experiment with new approaches, and iteratively improve your campaigns.

- **A/B Testing**: A/B testing involves comparing two versions of a message or campaign to determine which one performs better. Use analytics to set up controlled tests, varying elements like message content, timing, or CTA. By systematically testing different approaches, you can identify the most effective strategies and implement them more broadly.

- **Iterative Improvement**: Marketing is an ongoing process, and even successful campaigns can be improved. Regularly review your analytics to identify opportunities for fine-tuning your strategy. This might involve minor adjustments, such as tweaking the wording of a message, or more significant changes, like revamping your entire content approach.

Aligning with Business Goals

Finally, it's important to ensure that you're WhatsApp marketing strategy remains aligned with your overall business goals. Analytics not only help you improve campaign performance but also ensure that your efforts are contributing to broader objectives.

- **Goal Tracking**: Use analytics to track your progress toward specific business goals, such as increasing sales, generating leads, or improving customer satisfaction. Regularly review these metrics to ensure that your WhatsApp marketing efforts are driving the desired outcomes.
- **Adjusting Strategy Based on Business Needs**: As your business evolves, so too should your marketing strategy. Use analytics to adapt to changing business priorities, market conditions, and customer needs. For example, if your business is launching a new product, adjust your WhatsApp marketing strategy to focus on promoting that product and driving awareness among your target audience.

Analytics provide the foundation for a data-driven approach to WhatsApp marketing, enabling you to continuously refine and improve your strategy. By identifying strengths and weaknesses, refining audience targeting, optimizing timing and frequency, improving conversion paths, and aligning with business goals, you can make informed adjustments that enhance the effectiveness of your campaigns. This iterative process of analyzing, testing, and refining ensures that your WhatsApp marketing efforts remain dynamic, responsive, and ultimately successful in achieving your business objectives.

7.4 Reporting and Presenting Results to Stakeholders

Effectively communicating the outcomes of your WhatsApp marketing campaigns to stakeholders is crucial for securing continued support, demonstrating the value of your efforts, and aligning future strategies with business goals. This section will guide you through the process of creating clear, concise, and impactful reports that highlight key metrics, insights, and recommendations.

Identifying the Key Metrics to Report

The first step in reporting is selecting the most relevant metrics that will resonate with your stakeholders. While there are many metrics you could include, focus on those that align with your business objectives and the specific interests of your audience.

- **Engagement Metrics**: These include message open rates, response rates, and content interaction levels. Highlighting these metrics demonstrates how effectively your campaigns are capturing and maintaining audience attention.

- **Conversion Metrics**: Showcase metrics such as click-through rates (CTR), conversion rates, and the number of completed actions (e.g., purchases, and sign-ups). These metrics directly tie your WhatsApp marketing efforts to tangible business outcomes.
- **Return on Investment (ROI)**: ROI is often the most compelling metric for stakeholders, as it directly illustrates the financial impact of your campaigns. Presenting ROI helps stakeholders understand the profitability of your efforts.
- **Customer Feedback and Satisfaction**: If your campaigns include customer feedback elements, such as surveys or ratings, reporting on customer satisfaction (CSAT) scores can provide valuable insights into how your marketing efforts are perceived by your audience.

Structuring the Report

A well-structured report ensures that stakeholders can easily follow and understand the information presented. Consider the following structure when preparing your report:

- **Executive Summary**: Begin with a brief overview of the report's key findings, highlighting the most important results and insights. This section should provide a quick snapshot for stakeholders who may not have time to delve into the full report.
- **Campaign Overview**: Provide a concise description of the campaigns you're reporting on, including the objectives, target audience, and strategies used. This context is important for stakeholders to understand the goals and scope of your efforts.

- **Key Metrics and Results**: Present the key metrics in a clear and organized manner. Use visuals like charts, graphs, and tables to make the data more accessible and engaging. Ensure that each metric is accompanied by a brief explanation of what it represents and why it matters.
- **Analysis and Insights**: Offer an interpretation of the data, explaining what the results mean in the context of your campaign objectives. Highlight any significant trends, successes, or challenges that emerged. This section should provide stakeholders with a deeper understanding of the campaign's performance.
- **Recommendations**: Based on the analysis, provide actionable recommendations for future campaigns. Whether it's continuing a successful strategy, making adjustments to improve performance, or exploring new approaches, your recommendations should be clear and directly tied to the insights gained from the data.

Summarize the key takeaways from the report, reinforcing the main points and the overall impact of the campaigns. This final section should leave stakeholders with a strong understanding of the value your WhatsApp marketing efforts have brought to the business.

Using Visual Aids

Visual aids are powerful tools for making complex data more understandable and engaging. When reporting on WhatsApp marketing results, use a variety of visual elements to illustrate your points:

- **Charts and Graphs**: Use bar charts, line graphs, pie charts, and other graphical representations to show trends, comparisons, and proportions. For example, a line graph could effectively illustrate changes in engagement rates over time, while a pie chart might be used to show the distribution of different types of conversions.

- **Infographics**: Infographics combine data and visuals in a way that tells a story. They are particularly useful for summarizing key insights and making your report more visually appealing.
- **Screenshots and Examples**: Including screenshots of WhatsApp messages, campaign content, or analytics dashboards can provide stakeholders with concrete examples of your work and how it's being measured.

Presenting the Report

When presenting your report to stakeholders, consider the following best practices to ensure your presentation is clear, engaging, and impactful:

- **Tailor the Presentation to Your Audience**: Understand the specific interests and concerns of your audience. For example, a financial officer might be most interested in ROI, while a marketing director may focus on engagement metrics. Tailoring your presentation ensures that you're addressing the needs of each stakeholder.
- **Use Clear, Jargon-Free Language**: Avoid using technical jargon or marketing-specific terms that may not be familiar to all stakeholders. Clear, straightforward language helps ensure that your message is understood by everyone.
- **Focus on the Big Picture**: While it's important to provide detailed data, keep the presentation focused on the overall impact and key insights. Stakeholders are often more interested in what the data means for the business as a whole than in the granular details.

- **Encourage Questions and Discussion**: After presenting the report, invite stakeholders to ask questions and share their thoughts. This not only shows that you value their input but also provides an opportunity to address any concerns and clarify any points of confusion.
- **Follow Up with a Written Report**: After the presentation, provide stakeholders with a written version of the report. This allows them to review the information at their own pace and refer back to the data as needed.

Aligning Future Strategy with Stakeholder Feedback

One of the key benefits of reporting to stakeholders is the opportunity to gather feedback that can inform your future strategy. Pay attention to the questions, comments, and concerns raised during your presentation, as they can provide valuable insights into what stakeholders consider important.

- **Incorporating Feedback**: Use stakeholder feedback to refine your future campaigns. For example, if stakeholders express interest in exploring new content formats, consider experimenting with these in your next WhatsApp marketing efforts.
- **Setting Clear Objectives**: Based on the feedback and insights gained from the report, work with stakeholders to set clear objectives for future campaigns. This ensures that your WhatsApp marketing strategy remains aligned with the broader business goals.

Reporting and presenting the results of your WhatsApp marketing campaigns to stakeholders is a critical step in demonstrating the value of your efforts and securing ongoing support. By selecting relevant metrics, structuring the report effectively, using visual aids, and tailoring your presentation to your audience, you can communicate your campaign's impact clearly and convincingly. Additionally, by aligning future strategies with stakeholder feedback, you ensure that your WhatsApp marketing continues to drive meaningful business results.

Chapter 8: Advanced Techniques and Future Trends

As WhatsApp marketing continues to evolve, businesses that stay ahead of the curve by adopting advanced techniques and anticipating future trends will have a significant competitive advantage. This chapter explores cutting-edge strategies to optimize your WhatsApp marketing efforts and highlights emerging trends that are likely to shape the future of this powerful communication platform.

1. Leveraging AI and Chatbots

Artificial Intelligence (AI) and chatbots are revolutionizing the way businesses interact with customers on WhatsApp. By automating responses and personalizing communication, AI-driven tools can enhance customer experience while freeing up valuable resources.

- **Implementing AI-Powered Chatbots**: Chatbots can handle a wide range of tasks, from answering frequently asked questions to guiding users through a purchase process. Advanced AI chatbots can even analyze customer behavior and preferences to provide personalized product recommendations or support.
- **Personalization Through AI**: AI can analyze vast amounts of customer data to deliver highly personalized content and offers. For example, AI can help segment your audience based on their previous interactions, allowing you to send tailored messages that resonate with individual users.
- **24/7 Customer Support**: One of the significant advantages of chatbots is their ability to provide round-the-clock customer

support. This ensures that your customers can get the assistance they need at any time, enhancing customer satisfaction and loyalty.

2. Integrating WhatsApp with E-commerce

WhatsApp is increasingly becoming a vital channel for e-commerce businesses. By integrating WhatsApp with your e-commerce platform, you can streamline the buying process, improve customer support, and drive sales.

- **WhatsApp Business API for Transactions**: The WhatsApp Business API allows businesses to integrate their e-commerce systems directly with WhatsApp. This enables customers to browse products, receive order updates, and make purchases directly within the app.
- **Using WhatsApp for Order Confirmation and Tracking**: Sending order confirmations, shipping updates, and delivery notifications via WhatsApp provides customers with real-time information, enhancing their overall shopping experience.
- **Product Catalogs and Payments**: WhatsApp allows businesses to create product catalogs within the app, making it easy for customers to browse and shop. Additionally, the integration of payment options means that customers can complete transactions without leaving the chat, simplifying the buying process.

3. Interactive Content and Rich Media

As WhatsApp supports various media formats, businesses can create more engaging and interactive content to capture their audience's attention. Incorporating rich media into your marketing strategy can help differentiate your brand and improve customer engagement.

- **Rich Media Messaging**: Utilize images, videos, audio clips, and GIFs to create dynamic and visually appealing messages. Rich media can convey your message more effectively than plain text and can be particularly powerful in showcasing products, tutorials, or brand stories.
- **Interactive Polls and Surveys**: Engage your audience by using interactive features such as polls and surveys. These can be used to gather customer feedback, understand preferences, and involve customers in decisions like product development or content creation.
- **Gamification**: Introduce gamification elements into your WhatsApp marketing strategy, such as quizzes, challenges, or rewards programs. This not only makes the interaction more fun and engaging but can also drive higher participation and brand loyalty.

4. Security and Privacy Enhancements

As data privacy concerns continue to grow, businesses must prioritize security and privacy in their WhatsApp marketing efforts. Ensuring that customer data is handled securely and transparently will be essential for building and maintaining trust.

- **End-to-end Encryption**: WhatsApp's end-to-end encryption ensures that messages are only accessible to the sender and recipient, providing a secure communication channel. Businesses should emphasize this security feature to reassure customers about the safety of their data.

- **Data Privacy Compliance**: Stay informed about data privacy regulations such as GDPR and CCPA, and ensure that your WhatsApp marketing practices comply with these laws. This includes obtaining explicit consent for data collection and providing customers with clear options to manage their privacy settings.
- **Secure Payment Processing**: If your business uses WhatsApp for transactions, ensure that all payment processes are secure and compliant with industry standards. Partnering with reputable payment processors can help mitigate risks and provide customers with confidence in your brand.

5. Future Trends in WhatsApp Marketing

The landscape of WhatsApp marketing is continually evolving, and staying ahead of emerging trends is crucial for long-term success. This section explores some of the key trends that are likely to shape the future of WhatsApp marketing.

- **Increased Adoption of WhatsApp Commerce**: As more businesses recognize the potential of WhatsApp as a sales channel, WhatsApp Commerce is expected to grow. This will include more advanced features for product discovery, shopping, and payments within the app.
- **Expansion of WhatsApp Advertising**: While WhatsApp has traditionally been ad-free, there are indications that the platform may introduce more advertising opportunities in the future.

Businesses should stay alert to new ad formats and targeting options that could enhance their marketing reach.

- **Growth of Voice and Video Interactions**: With the increasing popularity of voice messages and video calls on WhatsApp, businesses will need to explore these formats for customer interaction. Whether it's providing customer support via video or sending personalized voice messages, these formats can create more authentic and engaging connections with customers.
- **AI and Machine Learning Integration**: As AI and machine learning technologies continue to advance, their integration into WhatsApp marketing will become more sophisticated. This could include more advanced predictive analytics, automated content creation, and deeper personalization based on real-time data.
- **Greater Focus on Community Building**: WhatsApp Groups and Communities are becoming more important as businesses seek to build closer relationships with their customers. Future trends may see businesses creating more niche groups, where customers can engage directly with brands and with each other, fostering a sense of community and loyalty.

As WhatsApp continues to evolve as a marketing platform, businesses that embrace advanced techniques and stay attuned to future trends will be well-positioned to succeed. Leveraging AI, integrating e-commerce, creating interactive content, prioritizing security, and anticipating future developments will enable you to harness the full potential of WhatsApp for your marketing efforts. By staying innovative and adaptable, you can ensure that your WhatsApp marketing strategy remains relevant, effective, and ahead of the competition.

8.1 Integrating WhatsApp with AI and Chatbots

Integrating WhatsApp with AI and chatbots is transforming the way businesses interact with customers, providing new opportunities for automation, personalization, and efficiency. As WhatsApp continues to grow as a primary communication channel, businesses that leverage AI-powered chatbots can significantly enhance their customer engagement, support, and marketing strategies. This section explores the benefits of integrating AI and chatbots with WhatsApp and provides insights into how to implement these technologies effectively.

The Role of AI in WhatsApp Marketing

Artificial Intelligence (AI) plays a crucial role in enhancing the capabilities of WhatsApp marketing by automating tasks, analyzing data, and providing personalized customer experiences. AI-driven chatbots can perform a variety of functions, from answering customer inquiries to offering tailored product recommendations, all while operating 24/7 without human intervention.

- **Automation of Repetitive Tasks**: One of the primary advantages of integrating AI with WhatsApp is the ability to automate repetitive tasks. Chatbots can handle common customer queries, process orders, schedule appointments, and send reminders, freeing up human resources for more complex tasks. This automation not only improves efficiency but also ensures that customers receive immediate responses, enhancing their overall experience.
- **Personalized Customer Interactions**: AI can analyze customer data, such as previous interactions, purchase history, and

preferences, to deliver highly personalized messages and offers. For example, a chatbot can recommend products based on a customer's browsing history or send personalized discount codes on their birthday. This level of personalization helps build stronger relationships with customers and increases the likelihood of conversions.

- **Predictive Analytics and Insights**: AI-powered chatbots can also use predictive analytics to anticipate customer needs and behaviors. By analyzing patterns in customer interactions, AI can predict which products a customer is likely to be interested in when they might need assistance, or what type of content they prefer. These insights enable businesses to proactively engage with customers, improving satisfaction and driving sales.

Implementing Chatbots on WhatsApp

Integrating chatbots with WhatsApp requires careful planning and execution to ensure that they meet the needs of both the business and its customers. The following steps outline how to effectively implement chatbots on WhatsApp.

- **Choosing the Right Chatbot Platform**: Several chatbot platforms offer integration with WhatsApp, each with its own set of features and capabilities. When selecting a platform, consider factors such as ease of use, scalability, AI capabilities, and integration with existing systems. Popular platforms include Twilio, ManyChat, and Dialogflow, each of which offers different levels of customization and functionality.
- **Defining Chatbot Functions and Use Cases**: Before implementing a chatbot, it's important to define its primary

functions and use cases. Will the chatbot handle customer service inquiries, assist with sales, or provide product recommendations? Clearly defining these functions will guide the development process and ensure that the chatbot meets business objectives.

- **Designing Conversational Flows**: The success of a chatbot largely depends on its ability to engage in natural, human-like conversations. Designing effective conversational flows involves mapping out the various paths a conversation might take, from greeting the customer to resolving their query. Consider incorporating natural language processing (NLP) to help the chatbot understand and respond to different ways customers might phrase their questions.

- **Testing and Optimization**: Once the chatbot is implemented, thorough testing is essential to ensure it functions correctly and provides a positive user experience. Test the chatbot with real users to identify any issues or areas for improvement. Continuously monitor the chatbot's performance and optimize its conversational flows, responses, and AI algorithms based on customer feedback and interaction data.

Enhancing Customer Support with Chatbots

One of the most common applications of chatbots on WhatsApp is in customer support. Chatbots can provide instant assistance to customers, resolving issues quickly and efficiently while reducing the workload on human support agents.

- **24/7 Availability**: Chatbots offer the significant advantage of being available around the clock, ensuring that customers can receive support whenever they need it. This is particularly valuable for businesses that operate in multiple time zones or have a global customer base. By providing immediate responses, chatbots help reduce customer wait times and improve overall satisfaction.

- **Handling High Volumes of Inquiries**: During peak periods, such as sales events or product launches, businesses may experience a surge in customer inquiries. Chatbots can handle large volumes of simultaneous interactions, ensuring that every customer receives timely assistance. This scalability is especially important for businesses looking to maintain high levels of service during busy times.

- **Seamless Escalation to Human Agents**: While chatbots are capable of handling many tasks, there are situations where a human touch is necessary. Effective chatbot implementation includes a seamless escalation process, where complex or sensitive inquiries are transferred to a human agent. This ensures that customers receive the appropriate level of support while still benefiting from the efficiency of AI.

Future Trends in AI-Driven WhatsApp Marketing

The integration of AI and chatbots with WhatsApp is expected to continue evolving, with new trends and technologies emerging that will further enhance the capabilities of businesses.

- **Advanced AI and Machine Learning**: As AI and machine learning technologies advance, chatbots will become even more sophisticated in understanding and predicting customer needs. This will lead to more accurate responses, better personalization, and a deeper understanding of customer behavior.

- **Voice-Activated Chatbots**: With the increasing popularity of voice assistants like Siri and Alexa, voice-activated chatbots are likely to become more common on WhatsApp. These chatbots will enable customers to interact with businesses through voice commands, providing a more convenient and hands-free experience.
- **Integration with IoT and Smart Devices**: As the Internet of Things (IoT) continues to grow, chatbots on WhatsApp may integrate with smart devices to offer more personalized and context-aware interactions. For example, a chatbot could remind a customer to reorder a product based on data from a connected device.

Integrating WhatsApp with AI and chatbots offers businesses a powerful way to automate tasks, personalize customer interactions, and enhance customer support. By carefully planning and implementing these technologies, businesses can improve efficiency, drive engagement, and stay ahead of the competition. As AI and chatbot technologies continue to evolve, staying informed about emerging trends will be key to maximizing the potential of WhatsApp as a marketing and communication platform.

8.2 Leveraging WhatsApp for E-commerce and Sales Funnels

WhatsApp is emerging as a powerful tool for e-commerce, offering businesses the ability to engage customers directly, streamline the buying process, and drive sales. With over 2 billion users worldwide, WhatsApp provides a unique opportunity to create personalized, real-time interactions that can significantly enhance the customer journey. In this section, we will explore how to effectively leverage WhatsApp for e-commerce and optimize sales funnels to maximize conversions.

WhatsApp as a Direct Sales Channel

WhatsApp's real-time, interactive nature makes it an ideal platform for facilitating direct sales. Unlike traditional e-commerce platforms, where interactions are often limited to browsing and purchasing, WhatsApp allows businesses to engage customers at every stage of the buying process, offering personalized support and guidance.

- **Product Catalogs and Direct Purchases**: WhatsApp Business enables businesses to create and share product catalogs directly within the app. These catalogs allow customers to browse products, view prices and read descriptions without leaving the chat. By integrating payment options, businesses can enable customers to make purchases directly from WhatsApp, streamlining the buying process and reducing friction.
- **Personalized Product Recommendations**: By analyzing customer interactions and preferences, businesses can use WhatsApp to deliver personalized product recommendations. For example, a customer who frequently purchases fitness products might receive a tailored message showcasing new arrivals in that category. This level of personalization can drive higher engagement and increase the likelihood of a sale.
- **Order Updates and Customer Support**: WhatsApp can also be used to enhance the post-purchase experience by providing real-time order updates, shipping notifications, and customer support. Customers can track their orders, receive delivery updates, and easily reach out to customer service if they have any issues. This

not only improves customer satisfaction but also fosters loyalty and repeat purchases.

Integrating WhatsApp into Sales Funnels

Sales funnels are a critical component of any successful e-commerce strategy, guiding potential customers through a series of steps from awareness to purchase. Integrating WhatsApp into your sales funnels can help you nurture leads more effectively and convert them into loyal customers.

- **Lead Generation and Qualification**: WhatsApp can be used as a tool for lead generation by encouraging potential customers to opt-in to receive updates and offers. For example, businesses can run ad campaigns on social media or their website that direct users to WhatsApp to sign up for exclusive deals. Once a lead is captured, chatbots or sales representatives can qualify the lead by engaging in conversation and gathering information about their needs and preferences.
- **Nurturing Leads with Targeted Messaging**: After capturing leads, WhatsApp can be used to nurture them through personalized, targeted messaging. Depending on where a lead is in the sales funnel, businesses can send relevant content, such as product demos, testimonials, or special offers, to move them closer to making a purchase. The interactive nature of WhatsApp allows for real-time engagement, making it easier to address any concerns or objections a lead may have.
- **Abandoned Cart Recovery**: One of the most effective ways to increase conversions is to address abandoned carts. WhatsApp can be used to send timely reminders to customers who have added

items to their cart but have not completed the purchase. These messages can include incentives like discounts or free shipping to encourage the customer to complete their purchase. By personalizing these reminders based on the specific items in the cart, businesses can significantly improve their abandoned cart recovery rates.

Creating an Effective WhatsApp Sales Strategy

To fully leverage WhatsApp for e-commerce and sales funnels, businesses need to develop a comprehensive sales strategy that aligns with their overall marketing goals. This involves setting clear objectives, understanding customer behavior, and continuously optimizing the approach based on performance data.

- **Setting Clear Objectives**: The first step in creating a WhatsApp sales strategy is to define clear objectives. Are you looking to increase sales, improve customer retention, or enhance customer support? Setting specific, measurable goals will help guide your strategy and ensure that your efforts are focused and effective.
- **Understanding Customer Behavior**: Understanding how your customers use WhatsApp is key to developing an effective sales strategy. Analyze customer interactions to identify common pain points, preferences, and behaviors. This information can help you tailor your messaging, content, and offers to better meet customer needs and drive conversions.
- **Continuous Optimization**: Like any sales strategy, your WhatsApp approach should be continuously optimized based on performance data. Track key metrics such as open rates, click-through rates, conversion rates, and customer satisfaction to

identify areas for improvement. A/B testing different messaging, content, and timing can also provide valuable insights into what works best for your audience.

Case Studies: Successful WhatsApp E-commerce Implementations

Many businesses have successfully leveraged WhatsApp to drive e-commerce sales, demonstrating the platform's potential as a powerful sales tool. Here are a few examples of how businesses have integrated WhatsApp into their sales funnels:

- **Case Study 1**: Fashion Retailer: A leading fashion retailer used WhatsApp to offer personalized styling advice to customers. By integrating a chatbot with their e-commerce platform, the retailer was able to recommend outfits based on customer preferences and past purchases. Customers could browse product catalogs, receive personalized recommendations, and complete their purchases directly within WhatsApp. This approach not only increased sales but also improved customer satisfaction and loyalty.
- **Case Study 2**: Health and Wellness Brand: A health and wellness brand used WhatsApp to recover abandoned carts and boost conversions. The brand sent personalized reminders to customers who had left items in their cart, offering a limited-time discount to encourage them to complete their purchases. This strategy resulted in a significant increase in conversion rates and reduced cart abandonment.
- **Case Study 3**: Electronics Company: An electronics company used WhatsApp to provide real-time customer support and product information during a major product launch. Customers could ask questions about the new product, receive detailed information, and

make a purchase directly through WhatsApp. The company also used the platform to send order updates and provide after-sales support, creating a seamless customer experience that drove high sales during the launch period.

Future Trends in WhatsApp E-commerce

As WhatsApp continues to evolve, new trends and technologies are emerging that will further enhance its role in e-commerce. Staying ahead of these trends will be essential for businesses looking to maximize the potential of WhatsApp as a sales channel.

- **WhatsApp Shops and In-App Payments**: The introduction of WhatsApp Shops and in-app payments is expected to further streamline the buying process, making it easier for customers to browse and purchase products without leaving the app. This will likely lead to increased adoption of WhatsApp as a primary sales channel, especially for small and medium-sized businesses.
- **Enhanced Personalization Through AI**: The integration of AI and machine learning into WhatsApp will enable even more advanced personalization. Businesses will be able to deliver highly targeted offers and recommendations based on real-time data, improving the customer experience and driving higher conversions.
- **Social Commerce Integration**: As social commerce continues to grow, WhatsApp is likely to play a key role in integrating social media and e-commerce. Businesses will be able to leverage WhatsApp to connect with customers on social platforms, drive traffic to their e-commerce sites, and close sales directly within the chat.

Leveraging WhatsApp for e-commerce and sales funnels offers businesses a powerful way to engage customers, streamline the buying process, and drive sales. By integrating WhatsApp into your sales strategy, you can create personalized, real-time interactions that enhance the customer journey and increase conversions. As the platform continues to evolve, staying informed about emerging trends and technologies will be key to maintaining a competitive edge and maximizing the potential of WhatsApp as a sales tool.

8.3 Exploring New Features: WhatsApp Pay, Catalogs, and More

WhatsApp continues to evolve as a powerful platform for businesses, regularly introducing new features that enhance its functionality for marketing, e-commerce, and customer engagement. Among the most significant of these are WhatsApp Pay, product catalogs, and several other tools designed to streamline business operations and improve customer experiences. In this section, we will explore these new features, their benefits, and how businesses can effectively integrate them into their strategies.

WhatsApp Pay: Simplifying Transactions

WhatsApp Pay is a game-changer for businesses, particularly in regions where mobile payments are rapidly becoming the norm. This feature allows users to send and receive money directly through the app, making transactions more convenient and seamless.

- **Integration with WhatsApp Business**: WhatsApp Pay is directly integrated with WhatsApp Business, allowing businesses to receive payments without the need for external payment gateways. This is particularly advantageous for small and medium-sized enterprises (SMEs) that may not have the resources to set up and manage complex payment systems. By using WhatsApp Pay, businesses can streamline the purchasing process, making it easier for customers to complete transactions.

- **Security and Trust**: Security is a critical concern for both businesses and customers in the realm of digital payments. WhatsApp Pay leverages the strong encryption that WhatsApp is known for, ensuring that transactions are secure and private. Additionally, the familiarity and trust that users already have in WhatsApp as a communication platform extend to WhatsApp Pay, making customers more comfortable using this method for transactions.

- **Boosting Sales Through Convenience**: The convenience of WhatsApp Pay can lead to increased sales, as customers are more likely to complete purchases when the process is quick and easy. By eliminating the need to switch between apps or enter lengthy payment details, WhatsApp Pay reduces friction in the buying process, leading to higher conversion rates.

Product Catalogs: Enhancing the Shopping Experience

Product catalogs are another powerful feature introduced by WhatsApp to support businesses, particularly those involved in e-commerce. These catalogs allow businesses to showcase their products directly within the app, providing a seamless shopping experience for customers.

- **Creating and Managing Catalogs**: Businesses can create product catalogs within WhatsApp Business by uploading images, descriptions, and prices for each product. These catalogs are easily accessible to customers within the chat, allowing them to browse products without leaving the conversation. This feature is especially useful for businesses that rely on personal interactions to drive sales, such as boutique shops or service providers.
- **Improved Customer Interaction**: Product catalogs enhance the way businesses interact with customers by making it easier to share product information. Instead of sending multiple images or links, businesses can simply share their catalog, allowing customers to view the entire range of products in one place. This streamlined approach not only improves the customer experience but also saves time for both the business and the customer.
- **Direct Purchases from Catalogs**: When integrated with WhatsApp Pay or other payment options, product catalogs can facilitate direct purchases. Customers can add items to their cart and proceed to checkout without leaving WhatsApp, making the entire shopping experience more convenient and efficient.

Other Emerging Features: Status Updates, QR Codes, and More

In addition to WhatsApp Pay and product catalogs, WhatsApp has introduced several other features that businesses can leverage to enhance their marketing and customer engagement strategies.

- **Status Updates for Business**: WhatsApp's Status feature, similar to Instagram Stories or Facebook Stories, allows businesses to share time-sensitive updates with their contacts. This can be used to promote limited-time offers, announce new product launches, or share behind-the-scenes content. Status updates are a powerful tool for creating urgency and engaging customers in a more informal, engaging way.

- **QR Codes for Easy Connections**: WhatsApp now allows businesses to generate QR codes that customers can scan to initiate a chat. This feature is particularly useful for offline marketing efforts, such as on business cards, flyers, or storefronts. By scanning the QR code, customers are instantly connected with the business on WhatsApp, making it easier to start conversations, ask questions, or make purchases.

- **Interactive Buttons and Call-to-Actions**: WhatsApp is also experimenting with interactive buttons and call-to-action (CTA) features that can be included in messages. These buttons allow customers to perform specific actions, such as making a purchase, booking an appointment, or visiting a website, directly from the chat. This functionality enhances the user experience by reducing the number of steps needed to complete an action.

Implementing New Features into Your Business Strategy

To fully benefit from these new WhatsApp features, businesses need to thoughtfully integrate them into their existing strategies. Here are some considerations for effectively using these tools:

- **Combining Features for Maximum Impact**: Many of WhatsApp's new features work best when used in combination. For example, businesses can use QR codes to drive traffic to their WhatsApp chat, share product catalogs to showcase their offerings and complete the sale with WhatsApp Pay. By creating a cohesive strategy that leverages multiple features, businesses can create a more seamless and engaging customer journey.

- **Educating Customers**: While these new features offer significant advantages, it's important to educate customers about how to use them. For instance, not all customers may be familiar with using WhatsApp Pay or accessing product catalogs. Providing clear instructions and support can help customers feel more comfortable and confident using these tools, leading to higher engagement and sales.

- **Continuous Testing and Optimization**: As with any new technology, it's essential to continuously test and optimize the use of these features. Monitor how customers are interacting with your WhatsApp catalog, how often they use WhatsApp Pay, and how effective your status updates are in driving sales. Use this data to refine your approach and improve the effectiveness of your WhatsApp marketing strategy over time.

Future Developments and Trends

As WhatsApp continues to innovate, businesses can expect to see even more features and tools designed to enhance e-commerce and customer engagement. Staying ahead of these trends and being early adopters of new features can give businesses a competitive edge.

- **Expanded E-commerce Capabilities**: WhatsApp is likely to continue expanding its e-commerce capabilities, potentially introducing more advanced catalog management tools, integration with other sales platforms, and enhanced payment options. Businesses that stay informed about these developments can leverage them to further streamline their sales processes and improve customer experiences.

- **Integration with Other Facebook Platforms**: Given that WhatsApp is owned by Meta (formerly Facebook), there is potential for deeper integration with other Meta platforms like Instagram and Facebook. This could allow businesses to create more unified marketing campaigns across multiple channels, using WhatsApp as a central hub for customer interaction and sales.

- **Enhanced AI and Automation Tools**: As AI technology continues to advance, businesses can expect to see more sophisticated automation tools integrated into WhatsApp. This could include more advanced chatbots, predictive analytics, and automated customer segmentation, all designed to improve the efficiency and effectiveness of WhatsApp marketing.

The introduction of features like WhatsApp Pay, product catalogs, and other tools has significantly expanded the platform's capabilities for businesses. By effectively integrating these features into your marketing and sales strategies, you can create more seamless, engaging, and efficient customer experiences. As WhatsApp continues to evolve, staying informed about new features and trends will be key to maintaining a competitive edge and maximizing the potential of this powerful platform.

8.4 The Future of WhatsApp Marketing: Predictions and Innovations

WhatsApp has rapidly evolved from a simple messaging app to a versatile platform for communication, commerce, and customer engagement. As businesses increasingly leverage WhatsApp for marketing, the platform is expected to introduce new features, integrate advanced technologies, and adapt to changing consumer behaviors. In this section, we will explore predictions and innovations that are likely to shape the future of WhatsApp marketing.

Increased Integration with Meta Ecosystem

As part of Meta's family of apps, WhatsApp is likely to see deeper integration with other platforms like Facebook, Instagram, and Messenger. This integration will enable businesses to create more cohesive marketing strategies across multiple channels, offering a unified customer experience.

- **Unified Messaging and Commerce**: Businesses might soon be able to manage customer interactions across WhatsApp, Messenger, and Instagram from a single platform. This would allow for seamless communication and the ability to track customer journeys across different channels. For example, a customer could inquire about a product on Instagram, receive a follow-up on WhatsApp, and complete a purchase on Facebook, all within a connected system.
- **Cross-Platform Ad Targeting**: Meta could introduce cross-platform ad targeting, where businesses can target users on WhatsApp based on their behavior on Facebook or Instagram. This would enhance the precision of marketing campaigns, allowing businesses to deliver highly relevant content to users on WhatsApp.

Advancements in AI and Chatbot Technology

Artificial Intelligence (AI) is expected to play a significant role in the future of WhatsApp marketing. As AI technology continues to advance, chatbots and other AI-driven tools will become more sophisticated, offering businesses new ways to engage with customers.

- **Enhanced Chatbots**: Future chatbots on WhatsApp will likely be more conversational and capable of handling complex customer queries. They may use natural language processing (NLP) to understand and respond to customer inquiries more accurately, providing a more personalized and human-like experience.
- **AI-Powered Customer Insights**: AI will enable businesses to gain deeper insights into customer behavior on WhatsApp. By analyzing interactions, AI can help businesses identify patterns, preferences, and pain points, allowing for more targeted marketing efforts. For example, AI could automatically segment customers based on their past interactions, enabling businesses to send personalized messages or offers.
- **Predictive Analytics**: AI could also be used to predict customer behavior, such as identifying which customers are most likely to make a purchase or churn. By leveraging predictive analytics, businesses can proactively engage with customers, offering incentives or support before they make a decision.

WhatsApp as a Comprehensive E-commerce Platform

As WhatsApp continues to expand its e-commerce capabilities, it is likely to become a more comprehensive platform for buying and selling products. This transformation will further blur the lines between communication and commerce, making WhatsApp a central hub for customer interactions.

- **Advanced Shopping Features**: WhatsApp may introduce advanced shopping features, such as product recommendations powered by AI, dynamic pricing based on customer behavior, and integration with augmented reality (AR) to allow customers to visualize products before purchasing. These features would enhance the shopping experience and drive higher engagement and sales.

- **Expanded Payment Options**: With the introduction of WhatsApp Pay, the platform has already begun facilitating transactions. In the future, WhatsApp could expand its payment options to include cryptocurrency payments, installment plans, or integration with digital wallets like Apple Pay or Google Pay. This would make the platform more versatile and accessible to a wider range of customers.

- **Social Commerce Integration**: WhatsApp is likely to play a key role in the growth of social commerce, where social interactions and e-commerce converge. Businesses could use WhatsApp to host live shopping events, where customers can browse products, ask questions, and make purchases in real time, all within the app.

Enhanced Privacy and Data Security Features

As concerns about data privacy continue to grow, WhatsApp will likely introduce new features to enhance user privacy and security. These innovations will be crucial for maintaining customer trust and ensuring compliance with global data protection regulations.

- **End-to-end Encryption for Business Messages**: While WhatsApp already uses end-to-end encryption for personal messages, it may extend this feature to business messages as well. This would provide an additional layer of security for sensitive customer information, such as payment details or personal data.
- **Data Minimization and Anonymization**: WhatsApp could implement data minimization and anonymization techniques to reduce the amount of personal data collected and stored by businesses. This would help businesses comply with regulations like GDPR and CCPA while protecting customer privacy.
- **Transparency and Control for Users**: WhatsApp may introduce features that give users more control over their data, such as the ability to view and manage the data that businesses collect about them, or to opt out of certain types of data processing. This would empower users to take control of their privacy and build trust with businesses.

WhatsApp as a Hub for Omnichannel Marketing

In the future, WhatsApp is likely to become a central hub for omnichannel marketing, where businesses can manage customer interactions across various platforms in a unified way. This will enable businesses to deliver a consistent and seamless experience, regardless of where the customer chooses to engage.

- **Integrated CRM Systems**: WhatsApp could integrate with customer relationship management (CRM) systems, allowing businesses to track and manage customer interactions across all channels. This would provide a 360-degree view of the customer, enabling more personalized and effective marketing campaigns.

- **Omnichannel Campaigns**: Businesses may be able to launch omnichannel marketing campaigns directly from WhatsApp, using the platform to coordinate messaging across email, social media, SMS, and other channels. This would ensure that customers receive consistent messaging and offers, regardless of how they interact with the brand.
- **Unified Customer Support**: WhatsApp could become a central hub for customer support, where businesses can manage and respond to customer inquiries across all channels in one place. This would streamline customer service operations and improve response times, leading to higher customer satisfaction.

Embracing the Metaverse and Virtual Reality

As Meta continues to develop the concept of the metaverse—a virtual world where users can interact in immersive environments—WhatsApp may play a role in this new frontier. The integration of virtual reality (VR) and augmented reality (AR) into WhatsApp could open up new possibilities for marketing and customer engagement.

- **Virtual Showrooms and Events**: Businesses could use WhatsApp to host virtual showrooms or events within the metaverse, where customers can explore products in 3D, interact with brand representatives, and make purchases in real time. This would create a more immersive and engaging shopping experience.
- **AR-Powered Product Demos**: WhatsApp could integrate AR features that allow customers to visualize products in their environment before making a purchase. For example, a customer could use their phone's camera to see how a piece of furniture

would look in their living room or how a pair of sunglasses would fit their face.

- **Virtual Customer Support**: In the metaverse, customer support could take on a new dimension, with virtual assistants or AI-driven avatars providing real-time help and guidance to customers. This would create a more interactive and personalized support experience.

The future of WhatsApp marketing is poised to be dynamic and innovative, with the platform likely to play an increasingly central role in business communication, commerce, and customer engagement. As WhatsApp continues to introduce new features and integrate with advanced technologies, businesses will have more opportunities to connect with customers in meaningful ways. By staying ahead of these trends and embracing the innovations that WhatsApp has to offer, businesses can create more effective marketing strategies, drive higher engagement, and ultimately achieve greater success in the digital age.

Conclusion

As we conclude this journey through the world of WhatsApp marketing, it's clear that this platform has evolved far beyond its origins as a simple messaging app. With its robust features and vast user base, WhatsApp offers unparalleled opportunities for businesses to connect with their customers in a direct, engaging, and impactful manner.

In this book, we have explored the essentials of WhatsApp marketing—from setting up your business profile and crafting effective strategies to leveraging advanced features and measuring success. Each chapter has provided a comprehensive guide to harnessing the power of WhatsApp for your marketing campaigns, ensuring you can create personalized, responsive, and effective interactions with your audience.

The Power of WhatsApp in Modern Marketing

WhatsApp's unique position as a ubiquitous communication tool allows businesses to break through the noise and engage with customers in a more personal and immediate way. Its integration of messaging, voice, video, and even payment functionalities creates a multifaceted platform that can drive not just communication but also transactions and customer loyalty. The key to leveraging WhatsApp's power lies in understanding its features, strategically planning your campaigns, and continuously optimizing your approach based on performance data.

The Importance of a Strategic Approach

Building a successful WhatsApp marketing strategy requires careful planning and execution. Defining your target audience, crafting relevant content, and setting clear objectives are crucial steps in creating a strategy that resonates with your audience. Integrating WhatsApp with your overall marketing efforts ensures that your campaigns are cohesive and aligned with your broader goals. Furthermore, respecting legal and ethical considerations helps maintain trust and credibility with your audience.

Engagement and Personalization

Effective WhatsApp marketing hinges on the ability to engage and personalize interactions with your customers. Growing your subscriber base, using WhatsApp groups and broadcasts, and handling inquiries with care is essential for building a loyal and responsive audience. Personalization techniques, such as targeted messaging and interactive content, enhance customer experiences and drive higher engagement rates.

Innovative Features and Future Trends

As WhatsApp continues to introduce new features and innovations, staying ahead of these trends is vital for maintaining a competitive edge. From WhatsApp Pay and product catalogs to AI-driven chatbots and integration with the Meta ecosystem, the platform's evolving capabilities offer exciting opportunities for businesses. Embracing these advancements and adapting your strategy accordingly will help you leverage WhatsApp's full potential and achieve sustained success.

Continuous Improvement

The dynamic nature of digital marketing requires businesses to be adaptable and proactive. Regularly analyzing performance metrics, conducting A/B testing, and adjusting your strategy based on insights will ensure that your WhatsApp marketing efforts remain effective and relevant. The ability to respond to changes in customer behavior and technology will be key to long-term success.

Final Thoughts

WhatsApp marketing is not just about using a new tool but about transforming the way you connect with your customers. It's about creating meaningful interactions, fostering trust, and delivering value through every message and campaign. By applying the principles and strategies outlined in this guide, you are well-equipped to navigate the exciting possibilities that WhatsApp offers.

As you embark on your WhatsApp marketing journey, remember that success comes from understanding your audience, leveraging the platform's features effectively, and continually refining your approach. With dedication and strategic insight, you can harness the power of WhatsApp to build stronger customer relationships, drive sales, and achieve your marketing goals.

Thank you for joining us on this exploration of WhatsApp marketing. Here's to your success in harnessing the power of WhatsApp to transform your marketing strategy and create exceptional experiences for your customers.

www.ingramcontent.com/pod-product-compliance
Lightning Source LLC
Chambersburg PA
CBHW082105220526
45472CB00009B/2053

* 9 7 9 8 3 4 5 2 7 8 6 6 6 *